Main Street

A Tasteful Passage
through Historic Franklin

A cookbook presented by
The Junior Auxiliary of Franklin

Junior Auxiliary Prayer

Send us, O God, as Thy messengers to the hearts without
a home, to lives without love, to the crowds without a guide. Send
us to the children whom none have blessed, to the famished
whom none have visited, to the fallen whom none have lifted, to
the bereaved whom none have comforted.

Kindle Thy flame on the altars of our hearts, that others may
be warmed thereby; cause Thy light to shine in our souls, that others
may see the way, keep our sympathies and insight ready, our wills keen,
our hands quick to help others in their need.

Grant us clear vision, true judgement, with great daring as we
seek to right the wrong; and so endow us with cheerful love that we may
minister to the suffering and forlorn even as Thou wouldst. May the
blessing of God Almighty, the Father, the Son and the Holy Spirit, rest
upon us and upon all our work. May He give us light to guide us, courage
to support us and love to unite us now and forever more.

Amen

This cookbook is a collection of favorite recipes, which are not necessarily
original but have been kitchen tested by the Publisher.

Published by Junior Auxiliary of Franklin

Copyright 1996 Junior Auxiliary of Franklin
P.O. Box 541
Franklin, Tennessee 37065-0541

ISBN: 0-9653965-0-9
Library of Congress Number: 96-78060

Edited, Designed and Manufactured by:
Favorite Recipes® Press
P.O. Box 305142
Nashville, Tennessee 37230
1-800-358-0560

Manufactured in the United States of America
First Printing: 1996   10,000 copies

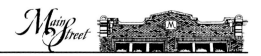

Foreword

Main Street. Seems every town has one. It's where many of our town began, and where homes and businesses grew side by side, upstairs and downstairs. It was where neighbors went to conduct their business, make their purchases, legislate and adjudicate, worship, meet and greet. It was the center of it all; a short walk home for a meal in the middle of the day and after business was concluded. Main Streets were the first thread in the fabric of small town life in America.

Franklin's Main Street is just such a place. Once the heart of business and commerce in Williamson County, it is still a busy, vibrant part of our ever-growing community. And although it is often a place we pass on our way to somewhere else, it is also a destination unto itself. We still come here to shop, dine, bank, attend church, and more. And just two blocks off the square and farther west along Main Street, downtown living is once again fashionable and in high demand. Our Main Street is an integral part of who we are in Franklin, for it typifies the old-fashioned values we hold important: hard work, respect, dignity, neighborliness.

Those are the same values that drive Junior Auxiliary. Not every town has a JA chapter, but those that do are fortunate indeed. Our towns are immeasurably richer because we, a group of volunteer women, devote our time and donate our energy to improving the health, welfare and education of our community's children. Through our neighborliness we seek to instill in these children the timeless virtues of compassion, respect, dignity and hard work.

Your purchase of *Main Street* helps support our projects, and for that we thank you. As you enjoy these recipes we hope you will remember that you are helping us provide books and school supplies to children whose families cannot afford them; clothes and household items to victims of domestic violence who are starting over; tutoring and mentoring to disadvantaged kids; scholarships to young women who plan careers in child-related fields; and much more. Your support means that we will continue to be an important thread in the fabric of Franklin's life.

I have become possessed by the spirit of venerable places that have had the dignity to survive.
Jenny Walton

Junior Auxiliary of Franklin History

Junior Auxiliary of Franklin is a nonprofit volunteer service
organization of women dedicated to improving the health,
welfare and education of families in Williamson County, particularly
those with children at risk of developing health, educational
or behavioral problems.

JAF is a chapter of the National Association of Junior Auxiliaries, Inc.,
a national organization chartered in Greenville, Mississippi, in 1941. The
Franklin Chapter was organized in 1981. The following account of our
early years is from a very special charter member.

*Our first president was Libby Isaacs Rawlings and what a lady
she was! She had all the confidence in the world in us. Sometimes we
had to wonder if we could do all that Libby dreamed for us.
She always said, "We CAN do it!" Her confidence gave us
inspiration and enthusiasm.*

*We started out with about forty members. Our goal was to be the
organization that our community could count on and turn to for their
needs. We lost about twenty members after they realized this was
not a social group but an organization of women who would be working
to serve this community. We held together and worked extra hard.
All projects were mandatory.*

*Our first order of business was to survey our community for needs. We
established a list of proposed projects. We had bake sales, fashion shows, etc.,
to raise money for these projects but quickly realized we needed big
money and a steady income to support our projects. That's when
Libby said, "We can do a cookbook."*

My best memories of the cookbook were of the many times we got together to proof recipes. It brought us much closer as a membership and as friends. Libby and her husband, Lenox, spent many hours proofing recipes in bed into the wee hours of the night until they both fell asleep. Lenox was the most supportive Junior Auxiliary husband.

The commitment and printing cost were really frightening to us all. Ten members signed a personal note for one hundred cookbooks and we held our breath.

To introduce our cookbook, we had a Feast and Fashion Show and a Tea at Carnton Mansion. That year we sold or gave a cookbook to everyone we knew. One of our members even sent a bill with her cookbook to all of her sorority sisters.

One of the finest assets of our beautiful community was the very unique collection of wonderful, charming hostesses and cooks in Franklin. By sharing them and their recipes with everyone we were truly "Flaunting Our Finest."

Over the last fourteen years, the organization's projects have been financed by proceeds from the sale of *Flaunting Our Finest.* This year the organization voted to begin work on a new cookbook with all-new recipes. We hope that you will enjoy *Main Street* and know that your support allows Junior Auxiliary of Franklin to continue the mission that the Charter members started, of assisting families as they struggle to provide the basic necessities of life for their children.

*F*or me there is no
truer window on the past
than the stories that
old homes tell.
Jenny Walton

Steering Committee

Jan Carlton
Jennifer Franklin
Kim Premo
Rhonda Wallace
Beth Wieck

The Steering Committee wishes to acknowledge our husbands for
their encouragement and patience. Without their support and love we
could not have accomplished our vision.

Frank Carlton
Dennis Franklin
Ken Premo
Tim Wallace
Adam Wieck

The committee would also like to extend our sincerest thanks to
all the members of Junior Auxiliary of Franklin. We appreciate all the
efforts and fellowship of the Lunch Bunch and Supper Club groups;
together we tested approximately four hundred recipes. We know you will
always remember our time spent together working on *Main Street*, the
cookbook that will make a difference in the lives of families in
Williamson County for many years to come.

What fun we had making our dream a reality!

Special thanks for giving of their time:
Macie Carder
René Evans—Foreword
Elaine Fox
Ernie and Lorraine Johnson
Cathy McKnight
Cheryl Warden
Rick Warwick

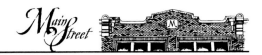

Junior Auxiliary of Franklin Membership

Active Members

Susan Brent
Nancy Brubaker
Macie Carder
Jan Carlton
Elise Crouch
Christine D'Eramo
Cyndi Echols
René Evans
Christine Feemster
Elaine Fox
Jennifer Franklin
Lisa Grainger
Lisa Gregory
Julia Halford
Delores Harley
Pam Horne
Stephanie Keffer
Elecia Lewis

Jackie Logan
Tina Luna
Marie Morris
Angie Orr
Kathryn Petit
Kim Premo
Sheila Priest
Leslie Saine
Karen Schumacher
Lisa Sessions
Debbie Sims
Melody Sipes
Joan Smith
Margie Thessin
Heidi Triggs
Cheryl Warden
Beth Wieck

Associate Members

Mona Brown
Leean Cherry
Ann Crocker
Barbara Dray
Bettye Embry

Tammy Gibbs
Jill Hall
Cathy McKnight
Connie Watson

Life Members

Mary Jane Anderson
Cindy Barraza
Sheila Bates
Sharon Blair
Sherri Darnell
Ann DeVan
Jackie Hardy
Susan Lane
Alice Lovvorn
Lucy Milton

Carla Myers
Susan Perkinson
Terri Petway
Mindy Schilling
Sara Seiberling
Kim Stewart
Jennifer Thomas
Rhonda Wallace
Vicki York

The Past Belongs to the Future, But Only the Present Can Preserve It.

HERITAGE FOUNDATION

The Heritage Foundation

The Heritage Foundation of Franklin and Williamson County is a twenty-eight-year-old preservation organization whose mission is the protection and preservation of the architectural, geographic, and cultural heritage of Franklin and Williamson County.

The Foundation has a membership of over eight hundred people. Each year the Foundation sponsors the Town & Country Tour of homes in May and the Heritage Ball in September. Preservation awards are given annually by the Foundation and the Williamson County Historical Society. The services it provides include:

The Heritage Classroom

Last year the Heritage Foundation provided programs in local history to ten thousand school children. The program has just been adopted by the Junior Auxiliary and the Foundation looks forward to working with this dynamic group of ladies.

Private Sector Initiatives

The Heritage Foundation recently purchased Roper's Knob, a sixty-seven-acre Civil War overlook located at the corner of the Mack Hatcher By-Pass and U.S. 31 South. Roper's Knob was used as a signal post during the Civil War and the original earthworks are still in place. Roper's Knob will be given to the City of Franklin to be used as a passive park.

National Register Nominations

The Heritage Foundation continually seeks to list properties on the National Register. In 1988 the Foundation was awarded a matching grant by the Tennessee Historical Commission to prepare a Multiple Resource National Register Nomination for Williamson County. This added eighty-one structures and historic sites, an extension of the Downtown Historic District and the Lewisburg Avenue Historic District to the National Register. Presently, the Foundation is working with the Center for Historic Preservation to add even more properties to the National Register.

Public Sector Initiatives

The Heritage Foundation works on a continuous basis to affect public policy in regard to historic sites, structures, landscapes and community character. The Foundation invites all interested people to join it in saving our architectural, geographic and cultural heritage.

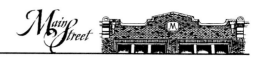

Contents

The days may come the days may go, but still the Hands of memory weave the blissful dreams of long days ago.
George Cooper

Patrons

We wish to thank all of our patrons. With their generous contributions they help to defray the cost of our cookbook, which allows us to put more back into the community we love.

Main Street
Sam Causey Photography Gallery
Ken and Kim Premo
Tim and Rhonda Wallace

First Avenue (formerly East Margin)
Dennis and Jennifer Franklin

Second Avenue (formerly Cameron Street)
RSS Ventures, Company
Jim and Nancy Brubaker
Frank and Jan Carlton—Carlton Insurance
Crouch Engineering, P.C.
Parisian

Third Avenue (formerly Main Cross)
CRS Appraisal Services, Inc.
Junior Cotillion, Williamson County Chapter—Sara Seiberling
P. Michael and Barbara Dray
First Tennessee Bank
Horner Rausch Optical (Hickory Hollow and Green Hills)
Dale and Jennifer Thomas

Appetizers

McEwen-German House

Appetizers

Bruschetta...13

Cheese Wafers...14

Claudia's Crabbies...14

Swedish Meatballs...15

Zesty Apricot Sauce...15

Marian's Mushrooms...16

Mushroom Puffs...17

Peppered Pecans...17

Salmon-Stuffed New Potatoes...18

Spinach and Prosciutto Horseshoe...19

Stuffed Cherry Tomatoes...19

Ruth's Beefy Cheese Ball...20

Strawberry Cheese Ring...20

Artichoke Pizza Dip...21

Pepperoni Pizza Dip...21

Reuben Casserole Dip...22

Cajun Shrimp Bake...22

Deviled Shrimp Spread...23

Texas Caviar...23

Tennessee Sin...24

McEwen-German House

This is an Italianate brick structure which was designed and constructed by John W. Miller, a contractor from Birmingham, in 1870.

It was built for Adelicia McEwen and her husband, Dr. Daniel German, by her parents, John Brown and Cynthia Graham McEwen. At the time this house was built, an elaborate garden that was a Franklin landmark separated Adelicia's home from that of her parents. This was quite an exquisite home for the era immediately following the Civil War.

This home stayed in the German-McEwen family until the early 1950s, when it was purchased to become Franklin's Public Library, War Memorial Library. After the library moved to its present location, the building was bought by private businesses.

The McEwen-German House is at 123 Fifth Avenue North and is currently occupied by the Law Offices of Hartzog, Silva & Davies, and Trans Financial Bank.

Bruschetta

These are not only a great appetizer but also a great accompaniment for salad or soup. When fresh tomatoes are in season, try omitting the artichokes.

1 cup chopped artichoke hearts
1 cup drained chopped fresh tomatoes
$1/4$ cup chopped onion
3 cloves of garlic, minced
2 tablespoons olive oil
$4^1/2$ teaspoons balsamic vinegar
$1/2$ teaspoon pepper
1 loaf French bread
Freshly grated Parmesan cheese

Combine the artichoke hearts, tomatoes, onion, garlic, olive oil, vinegar and pepper in a bowl; mix lightly. Slice the bread diagonally into 1 inch thick slices. Spread the tomato mixture on the bread slices. Sprinkle the Parmesan cheese on top. Place on a baking sheet. Bake at 375 degrees for 10 to 15 minutes or until lightly toasted. Serve while hot and crusty.
Yield: 24 servings.

For many years you could buy all of the goods that you needed right on Main Street. There were tailors, cobblers, green grocers, butchers, confectioners, furniture stores, dry goods stores, farm implements, jewelers, tobacconists, and druggists.

Cheese Wafers

8 ounces sharp Cheddar cheese
1/2 cup butter or margarine
1 1/2 cups all-purpose flour
1 cup finely chopped pecans

Shred the cheeses finely while cold. Place the cheeses and butter in a large bowl and let stand until softened. Add the flour and pecans and mix well. Divide into 3 portions. Shape each portion into a log and wrap in waxed paper. Chill the logs overnight. Slice the logs into 1/4-inch-thick wafers and arrange the wafers on a baking sheet; do not allow the wafers to touch. Bake at 425 degrees for 10 minutes or until light brown. Cool the wafers on the baking sheet for 1 to 2 minutes and remove to a wire rack to cool completely.
Yield: 6 dozen.

Claudia's Crabbies

1/2 cup butter
1 (6-ounce) jar Old English cheese spread
1 1/2 teaspoons mayonnaise-type salad dressing
1/2 teaspoon minced fresh garlic
1/2 teaspoon seasoned salt
6 ounces fresh or frozen crab meat, finely chopped
6 English muffins, split

Melt the butter. Combine with the cheese spread, salad dressing, garlic and seasoned salt in a bowl and mix well. Drain the crab meat well. Add to the cheese mixture and mix well. Spread the mixture over the muffin halves. Arrange on a baking sheet. Cut each muffin half into 6 wedges. (To freeze unbaked crabbies, store, tightly wrapped, until needed.) Place the wedges on a baking sheet. Bake in a preheated 450-degree oven for 10 minutes or until golden brown. Serve hot.
Yield: 6 dozen.

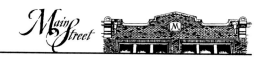

Swedish Meatballs

Plan to double the meatballs and the sauce—everyone loves them so one recipe is not enough.

2 pounds ground chuck
2 slices bread
1 1/2 envelopes onion soup mix
Zesty Apricot Sauce (see below)

Place the ground chuck in a medium bowl. Sprinkle the bread with water. Let the bread stand until completely moistened then squeeze out excess moisture. Add the bread and soup mix to the ground chuck and mix well. Shape the mixture into small balls and arrange in a shallow baking pan sprayed with nonstick cooking spray. Bake the meatballs at 350 degrees for 20 minutes or until cooked through, turning as necessary; drain well. Place the meatballs in a large saucepan. Add the Zesty Apricot Sauce. Simmer until heated through. The meatballs may be frozen before cooking if desired.
Yield: 3 to 4 dozen.

Zesty Apricot Sauce

1 cup catsup
1 cup apricot nectar
8 teaspoons vinegar
8 teaspoons brown sugar
4 teaspoons prepared horseradish
2 teaspoons Worcestershire sauce

Combine the catsup, apricot nectar, vinegar, brown sugar, horseradish and Worcestershire sauce in a saucepan. Bring to a simmer, stirring frequently. Simmer for 10 minutes.

Main Street also offered every type of service imaginable. You could find a barber, blacksmith, doctor, dentist, photographer, wagon repairman, broom maker, and even a pawnbroker without venturing off Main Street.

*E*ntertainment and dining were found on Main Street. There were several hotels and restaurants, a pie wagon, a pool hall, and a movie theatre. At one time there was a gambling establishment and, during the days of segregation, there was a black nightclub.

Marian's Mushrooms

1 link hot and spicy Portuguese or Italian sausage, finely chopped
1/2 purple onion, chopped
2 cloves of garlic, minced
1 red bell pepper, chopped
1 jalapeño, chopped (optional)
1/2 can Italian bread crumbs
1 to 2 cups chopped fresh crab meat
Seasoned salt and pepper to taste
2 cups shredded Monterey Jack cheese
1 egg, beaten
24 (or more) mushroom caps

Sauté the sausage with the onion, garlic, red pepper and jalapeño
in a skillet until the sausage is brown and the onion is tender;
drain well. Add the bread crumbs, crab meat and seasonings and mix well.
Remove from the heat. Add the cheese and mix until the cheese
melts. Add the egg and mix well. Stuff the mushroom caps with the crab
meat mixture; arrange on a lightly buttered baking sheet. Bake at
375 degrees for 15 to 20 minutes or until hot and bubbly. Serve hot. For
even spicier stuffing, use Monterey Jack cheese with jalapeños.
Yield: 2 dozen.

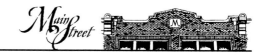

Mushroom Puffs

2 (8-count) cans crescent rolls
8 ounces cream cheese, softened
1 (4-ounce) can mushrooms, drained, chopped
2 green onions, chopped
1 teaspoon seasoned salt
1 egg, beaten
2 tablespoons poppy seeds

Unroll the dough on a lightly floured work surface. Shape into
a large rectangle by pressing the edges and perforations together to seal.
Combine the cream cheese with the mushrooms, green onions
and seasoned salt in a bowl and mix well. Spread over the rectangle.
Roll up as for a jelly roll and seal edge. Cut into 1-inch slices and arrange
cut side down on a lightly greased baking sheet. Brush with the
beaten egg and sprinkle with the poppy seeds. Bake at 375
degrees for 10 minutes or until golden brown. Serve hot.
The puffs may be frozen before baking if desired.
Yield: 2 1/2 dozen.

Peppered Pecans

3 tablespoons butter
3 cloves of garlic, minced
1 tablespoon Tabasco sauce
1/2 teaspoon salt
3 cups pecan halves

Melt the butter in a large skillet. Add the garlic, Tabasco sauce and salt.
Cook for 1 minute, stirring constantly. Add the pecans and
toss in the butter mixture until coated. Spread in a single layer on a
baking sheet. Bake at 250 degrees for 1 hour or until the
pecans are crisp, stirring occasionally.
Yield: 3 cups.

*Most of the
businesses on Main Street
had apartments in their
second stories. The
merchants and tradesmen
lived above their places
of business. Later, many of
them built fine homes
on Franklin's tree-lined
side streets.*

Salmon-Stuffed New Potatoes

12 baby red-skinned new potatoes
1 tablespoon olive oil
3^1/$_2$ ounces smoked salmon, finely chopped
2 tablespoons sour cream
2 teaspoons minced red onion
1 teaspoon drained capers
^{1}/$_2$ teaspoon prepared horseradish
Pepper to taste

Scrub the potatoes and cut into halves crosswise. Place the olive oil in a bowl. Add the potatoes and mix until the potatoes are coated with olive oil. Place the potatoes cut side down on a large heavy baking sheet. Bake the potatoes at 400 degrees for 25 minutes or just until tender. Let stand until completely cooled. Combine the salmon, sour cream, onion, capers and horseradish in a small bowl. Season with the pepper. Cut a small slice from the rounded side of each potato to form a base; place potatoes base side down on a serving platter. Scoop out about a teaspoon of pulp from the center of each potato with a melon baller or small spoon. Fill the cavity with the salmon mixture. Garnish with a sliver of additional smoked salmon and a caper. Chill, covered, for up to 2 hours before serving. May prepare the potatoes and salmon mixture a day ahead, chill separately and assemble before serving.
Yield: 2 dozen.

Spinach and Prosciutto Horseshoe

1 loaf frozen bread dough
5 ounces fresh spinach (not frozen)
5 to 6 ounces prosciutto
8 ounces basil and tomato feta cheese
(or plain feta with Italian seasoning)

Let the bread dough thaw overnight in the refrigerator. Let rise. Roll the dough on a lightly floured surface into a long rectangle about 8 inches wide. Rinse spinach leaves, discard stems and pat dry. Microwave spinach for 1 minute and pat dry again. Arrange overlapping layers of the spinach leaves and prosciutto lengthwise on half the dough rectangle. Crumble the cheese over the layers. Fold the dough over to enclose the filling and press the dough edges to seal. Cut several 1-inch slits in the top to vent. Shape into a horseshoe on a lightly greased baking sheet. Bake at 375 degrees for 20 to 30 minutes or until golden brown. Slice into servings. Serve hot.
Yield: 18 to 20 servings.

Stuffed Cherry Tomatoes

36 cherry tomatoes
11 ounces cream cheese, softened
2 tablespoons mayonnaise
1 envelope ranch salad dressing mix
Alfalfa sprouts
Snipped fresh parsley

Rinse the tomatoes and cut into halves. Scoop out the pulp using a melon baller or small spoon and invert the tomato halves to drain. Mix the next 3 ingredients in a bowl. Spoon into a sealable plastic bag. Chill for 3 hours to overnight to blend flavors. Arrange the tomato halves cut side up on a bed of alfalfa sprouts. Snip the corner from the plastic bag. Pipe the cream cheese mixture from the plastic bag to fill the tomato halves. Garnish with a sprinkle of snipped parsley.
Yield: 6 dozen.

Ruth's Beefy Cheese Ball

*This cheese ball is also delicious made with corned beef
and served with rye crackers or thinly sliced bread.*

24 ounces cream cheese, softened
2 (3-ounce) packages wafer sliced beef
2 to 3 tablespoons Worcestershire sauce
2 tablespoons MSG (optional)
1 bunch green onions, chopped

Beat the cream cheese in a mixer bowl until light. Finely chop the beef
from one of the packages. Add to the cream cheese. Add the
Worcestershire sauce, MSG and green onions; mix well. Shape into a
ball. Wrap the ball in the remaining beef. Wrap tightly and chill
until serving time. Serve with crackers.
Yield: 1 large cheese ball.

Strawberry Cheese Ring

16 ounces each extra-sharp and medium Cheddar cheese
$^1/_3$ cup chopped green onions
1 cup (or more) mayonnaise
1 teaspoon red pepper flakes
1 cup chopped pecans
Strawberry preserves

Shred the cheeses finely. Combine the cheeses with the green onions in a
large bowl. Add enough mayonnaise to bind the mixture together. Sprinkle
with red pepper. Lightly oil a 7-cup ring mold and sprinkle with $^1/_4$ cup of
the pecans. Press the cheese mixture into the mold. Chill until firm.
Unmold the cheese ring onto a serving platter. Pat the remaining pecans
over the surface of the cheese. Fill the center with strawberry preserves.
For a variation, substitute pepper jelly for the strawberry preserves.
Yield: 1 large cheese ring.

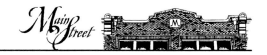

Artichoke Pizza Dip

1 (12-ounce) can artichoke hearts
1/2 cup grated Parmesan cheese
12 ounces shredded mozzarella cheese
1 cup mayonnaise
1/2 cup sliced jalapeños

Drain and chop the artichokes. Combine the artichokes with
the cheeses, mayonnaise and jalapeños in a bowl and mix well. Spoon into a
lightly greased baking dish. Bake at 350 degrees for 20 minutes
or until brown and bubbly. Serve hot with assorted favorite crackers or
other favorite dippers. The dip may be prepared the day before and baked
just before serving or may be reheated in the microwave.
Yield: 8 to 10 servings.

Pepperoni Pizza Dip

8 ounces cream cheese, softened
1/2 cup sour cream
1 teaspoon oregano
1/8 teaspoon garlic powder
1/8 teaspoon cayenne
1/2 cup pizza sauce
1/2 cup finely chopped pepperoni
1/4 cup each finely chopped green onions and green bell pepper
1/2 cup (or more) shredded mozzarella cheese

Combine the cream cheese, sour cream, oregano, garlic powder and cayenne
in a bowl and beat until smooth and creamy. Spread the mixture evenly in a
deep-dish pie plate or quiche pan. Add layers of the pizza sauce, pepperoni,
green onions and green pepper. Bake at 350 degrees for about 10 minutes.
Sprinkle the mozzarella cheese over the top. Bake for 10 minutes longer.
Serve hot with tostados or taco-flavored corn chips.
Yield: 8 to 10 servings.

In 1865 a Main Street merchant put out this advertisement to appeal to the frugal shopper: *Where can it be found? Adjoining the post office at the southwest corner of Main. What goods are the best? The best goods are always the cheapest.*

Reuben Casserole Dip

1 (16-ounce) can sauerkraut
1 (8-ounce) can corned beef
8 ounces Swiss cheese, finely shredded
8 ounces Cheddar cheese, finely shredded
1 cup mayonnaise

Drain the sauerkraut, rinse well and drain well. Chop the sauerkraut finely. Chop the corned beef finely. Combine the sauerkraut, corned beef and the shredded cheeses in a bowl. Add the mayonnaise and mix well. Spoon the mixture into a quiche plate or deep-dish pie plate. Bake at 350 degrees for 30 minutes or until heated through. Serve hot with party rye bread, wheat crackers and fresh vegetable dippers.
Yield: 12 to 15 servings.

Cajun Shrimp Bake

$^{1}/_{2}$ cup olive oil
$2^{1}/_{2}$ tablespoons Creole seasoning
2 tablespoons fresh lemon juice
3 tablespoons finely chopped parsley
1 tablespoon honey
1 tablespoon soy sauce
Cayenne to taste
1 pound uncooked shrimp, peeled, deveined

Combine the olive oil, Creole seasoning, lemon juice, parsley, honey, soy sauce and cayenne in a 9x13-inch baking dish and mix well. Add the shrimp and toss until the shrimp are coated with the mixture. Marinate the shrimp, covered, in the refrigerator for $1^{1}/_{2}$ hours. Bake, uncovered, at 450 degrees for about 12 minutes or until the shrimp turn pink, stirring occasionally; do not overcook. Serve the shrimp with lemon wedges and warm French bread.
Yield: 4 servings.

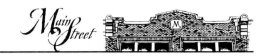

Deviled Shrimp Spread

1 pound cooked shrimp, peeled, deveined, finely chopped
8 ounces cream cheese, softened
$1/2$ cup mayonnaise
$1/4$ cup chili sauce
2 tablespoons freshly grated horseradish
1 each small onion and rib celery, chopped
Juice of 1 lemon
Tabasco sauce to taste
1 tablespoon minced fresh chives

Mix the first 9 ingredients in a bowl. Press into an oiled mold or shape into
a log. Chill, tightly covered, until firm. Unmold onto a serving platter.
Sprinkle with the chives. Serve with assorted crackers and fresh vegetables.
Yield: 12 servings.

Texas Caviar

1 (16-ounce) can black beans, drained
1 (16-ounce) can black-eyed peas with bacon and jalapeños, drained
1 (11-ounce) can Mexican corn, drained
1 (3-ounce) can sliced black olives, drained
1 (14-ounce) can chopped salsa-style tomatoes
1 large green bell pepper, chopped
$1/2$ large onion, chopped
10 pickled jalapeño slices, chopped
$3/4$ cup cilantro sprigs, chopped
Italian salad dressing to taste
Salt and pepper to taste

Combine the first 9 ingredients in a large bowl. Add the desired
amount of salad dressing and mix gently. Add the salt and pepper. Chill
in the refrigerator. Serve with Melba toast or tortilla chips.
Yield: 5 to 6 cups.

*C*ompetition among
Main Street merchants was
often fierce. One store owner
allegedly killed a competitor
who walked into his shop
with a metal file in his hand.

*M*ain Street usually boasted at least one coffin shop, but no funeral parlors. Visitation with the bereaved family took place in the front parlor of the family home. The man who patented metal burial vaults had his office in the Magli building on the square.

Tennessee Sin

With a name like this, it has to be good!

2 (16-ounce) loaves French bread
8 ounces cream cheese, softened
1 cup sour cream
1³/4 cups shredded Cheddar cheese
³/4 cup chopped cooked ham
¹/3 cup chopped green onions
¹/2 cup chopped green bell pepper
¹/4 teaspoon Worcestershire sauce
Paprika to taste

Cut the top one-fourth from one of the bread loaves. Scoop out the bread from the bottom portion, leaving a 1-inch-thick shell. Cut the top, scooped out bread portion and the remaining loaf into 1-inch cubes. Place the bread shell and the bread cubes on a large baking sheet. Bake at 350 degrees for 12 minutes or until lightly toasted. Beat the cream cheese in a bowl. Add the sour cream and beat until creamy. Add the cheese, ham, green onions, green pepper and Worcestershire sauce and mix well with a spoon. Spoon the mixture into the bread shell. Sprinkle with paprika. Wrap the filled shell in heavy-duty foil and place on a baking sheet. Bake at 350 degrees for 30 minutes. Unwrap the loaf. Place on a large serving platter. Surround the loaf with the toasted bread cubes and serve immediately.
Yield: 12 to 15 servings.

Beverages

Clouston Hall

Beverages

Slushy Banana Punch...27
Bourbon Slush...27
Champagne Punch...28
Lemon-Lime Punch...28
Peach Fuzz...28
Punch Mexican-Style...29
Red Roosters...29
Tea Punch...29
Slushy Wine Punch...30
Boiled Custard...30
Heavenly Coffee Punch...31
Hot Buttered Rum...31
Mulled Cider...32
Christmas Wassail...32

Clouston Hall

This beautiful Federal home was built between 1828 and 1840.
It was designed by Joseph Reiff. Similar in style to Carter
House, construction on Clouston Hall actually predates Carter House.
Although Clouston Hall seems far removed from the fierce
fighting during the Battle of Franklin, cannon shot flew overhead from
nearby Fort Granger and hundreds of wagons from the Union
Army filled the immediate area as they awaited completion of a hastily
built bridge across the Harpeth River. Dr. and Mrs. Daniel B.
Cliffe were longtime residents of this home. Dr. Cliffe's mother,
Cornelia (Ninne) Stith Nichols Cliffe, while in her teens,
is credited for taking a scuttle of coals covered with ashes and burning
the bridge over the Harpeth River, upon hearing that the
town was to be invaded by Yankees.

During some later restoration work Minié balls from the battle
fell from behind Clouston Hall's window frames.
The original smokehouse and kitchen no longer exist.

This home is located at 202 Second Avenue South, and has been
carefully preserved for over thirty years by its owner, Mr. Bunn Gray.

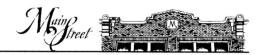

Slushy Banana Punch

2 cups sugar
3 cups water
1 (46-ounce) can pineapple juice
1^1/$_2$ cups orange juice
^{1}/$_4$ cup lemon juice
3 large bananas
3 quarts ginger ale, chilled
1 cup rum (optional)

Combine the sugar and water in a saucepan. Bring to a boil, stirring to dissolve the sugar. Reduce the heat and simmer for 20 minutes. Remove from the heat and set aside to cool. Combine the pineapple juice, orange juice and lemon juice in a large freezer container. Mash the bananas. Add the bananas and the sugar syrup to the juice mixture and mix well. Freeze until firm. Place the frozen juice mixture in a punch bowl. Add the chilled ginger ale and stir until slushy. Add the rum just before serving.
Yield: 48 small punch cups.

Bourbon Slush

1^3/$_4$ cups sugar
2 cups strong tea
7 cups water
1 (12-ounce) can each frozen orange juice and lemonade concentrate
2 cups bourbon
1 to 2 liters lemon-lime soda, chilled

Combine the sugar, tea and water in a large freezer container; stir until the sugar dissolves. Thaw the frozen orange juice and lemonade concentrates and add to the tea mixture; mix well. Stir in the bourbon. Freeze until firm. Spoon enough of the slush into old-fashioned glasses to fill ^{2}/$_3$ full. Add chilled lemon-lime soda to fill the glasses.
Yield: 15 to 20 servings.

Champagne Punch

1 (32-ounce) bottle cranberry juice cocktail, chilled
1 quart orange juice, chilled
1/2 cup each chilled lemon juice and sugar
1 (25.4-ounce) bottle chablis, chilled
2 (25.4-ounce) bottles Champagne, chilled

Mix the juices and sugar in a punch bowl until the sugar
dissolves. Add the chablis. Add the Champagne just before serving
and mix very gently. Garnish with orange slices.
Yield: 5 quarts.

Lemon-Lime Punch

1 envelope lemon or lime drink mix, prepared
1 (46-ounce) can pineapple juice
1 liter ginger ale
1/2 gallon lime sherbet

Freeze half the prepared drink mix in a 1-quart ring mold. Mix the
remaining drink mix with the juice and chill until serving time. Pour into a
punch bowl. Add the ginger ale and scoops of sherbet. Add the ice ring.
Yield: 4 quarts.

Peach Fuzz

3 soft ripe unpeeled peaches, cut into halves
1 (6-ounce) can frozen pink lemonade concentrate, thawed
3/4 cup vodka
Cracked ice cubes

Purée the peaches, concentrate and vodka in a blender. Add the ice. Process
until the ice is crushed. Pour into chilled glasses and serve with a straw.
Yield: 6 to 8 servings.

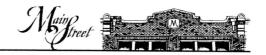

Punch Mexican-Style

6 cups sugar
14 cups water
1 (46-ounce) can orange juice
2 (46-ounce) cans pineapple juice
1 (6-ounce) can frozen lemonade concentrate, thawed
8 teaspoons almond extract
2 tablespoons vanilla extract

Dissolve the sugar in water in a large container with a tightly fitting lid. Add remaining ingredients. Freeze a portion of the punch in a ring mold. Chill the punch for 2 days or longer. Pour into a punch bowl. Add the ice ring.
Yield: 25 to 30 servings.

Red Roosters

1 quart each orange juice and lemonade
1 quart each vodka or rum, and cranberry juice cocktail
1 to 2 drops red food coloring (optional)

Mix ingredients in a gallon-size sealable plastic bag. Freeze for several hours. Thaw for 1¼ hours before serving. Pour into punch bowl; stir until slushy.
Yield: 1 gallon.

Tea Punch

3 cups each brewed tea, orange juice and pineapple juice
1 cup lemon juice
2 cups sugar
6 cups ginger ale

Mix the tea and juices in a large pitcher. Stir in the sugar until dissolved. Add the ginger ale just before serving. Pour over crushed ice in tall glasses.
Yield: 1 gallon.

The current Inman building on the square was originally the city hall. It contained the old jail, or "Calaboose," the police station, and the fire hall. The enormous old doors through which teams of horses used to race pulling the fire engines have been enclosed but are still visible.

Slushy Wine Punch

5 cups water
2¹/₂ cups sugar
1¹/₂ to 1³/₄ cups lemon juice
2 (46-ounce) cans unsweetened pineapple juice
Dry white wine

Combine the water and sugar in a stockpot. Heat until the sugar dissolves, stirring frequently. Remove from the heat. Add the lemon juice and pineapple juice and mix well. Pour into a large covered freezer container. Freeze for 4 hours or longer. Let stand until partially thawed. Pour into a punch bowl. Add the desired amount of white wine and stir until slushy.
Yield: about 1 gallon.

Boiled Custard

2 cups sugar
¹/₂ cup all-purpose flour
4 to 6 eggs, beaten
3 quarts milk
2 teaspoons vanilla extract

Mix the sugar and flour in a large saucepan. Add the eggs and blend well. Stir in the milk gradually. Cook over low heat until thickened to the desired consistency, stirring constantly. Remove from the heat and stir in the vanilla. Chill in a tightly covered container until serving time.
Yield: 3 to 3¹/₂ quarts.

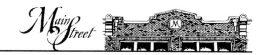

Heavenly Coffee Punch

2 cups sugar
2 cups water
2 ounces instant coffee powder
$^1/_2$ gallon vanilla ice cream
$^1/_2$ gallon chocolate ice cream
2 quarts milk

Combine the sugar and water in a large saucepan. Bring to a boil, stirring constantly. Add the coffee powder and stir until the coffee and sugar dissolves. Pour the mixture into an airtight container. Chill until serving time. Soften the ice creams in a punch bowl. Add the coffee mixture and milk and mix until well blended. Ladle into punch cups and garnish with a sprinkle of grated chocolate. May add chocolate liqueur.
Yield: 24 servings.

Hot Buttered Rum

1 cup apple cider
$^1/_3$ cup rum
1 teaspoon butter
2 cinnamon sticks
Ground cinnamon to taste

Heat the cider and rum in a heavy saucepan over medium heat for about 15 minutes. Pour into heavy mugs. Add $^1/_2$ teaspoon butter to each mug. Add a cinnamon stick and sprinkle of cinnamon to each.
Yield: 2 servings.

*I*n front of the courthouse was a fence where local men used to gather to whittle, chew, and gossip. This was called the Buzzard's Roost. Once a local prankster ran an electrical wire along the fence and waited for the Buzzards to perch. When they did, the prankster gave them a shock and sent them flying in all directions.

Franklin welcomes the holiday season with its "Dickens of a Christmas" celebration Costumed characters, carriage rides and the smell of roasting chestnuts are all a part of this popular annual event. Another holiday treat is the Carter House Candlelight Tour, which opens many of Franklin's beautiful homes to the public.

Mulled Cider

1/2 gallon apple cider or apple juice
1 cup orange juice
3 cinnamon sticks
1/2 cup packed brown sugar
1 teaspoon whole cloves
Cinnamon sticks and orange slices for garnish

Combine the cider, orange juice, cinnamon sticks and brown sugar in a large heavy saucepan. Place the cloves in a mesh tea basket and add to the cider mixture. Bring to a simmer over medium-low heat. Keep warm over low heat. Ladle into mugs
Yield: 8 to 10 servings.

Christmas Wassail

1 gallon apple cider
1 cup orange juice
6 tablespoons lemon juice
2 cups sugar
12 cinnamon sticks
48 whole cloves
1/4 cup whole allspice
4 cups apple brandy

Combine the cider, orange juice, lemon juice, sugar, cinnamon, cloves and allspice in a large heavy saucepan. Bring to a boil and reduce the heat to low. Simmer for 10 minutes. Strain the mixture and discard the spices. Add the brandy. Keep the wassail warm in a slow cooker. May place juices in a large party percolator and add the sugar and spices to the basket. Perk using the manufacturer's instructions and add the brandy to the perked liquid.
Yield: 24 to 30 servings.

Green-Moore House

Soups & Stews

Green-Moore House

The Green-Moore House can be found in the Hincheyville Historic District. While lots in Hincheyville were first offered for sale in 1819, the record was lost somewhere in the courthouse for 106 years, being registered for the first time in 1925. The first owner of the Green-Moore lot is recorded as Patrick Darby.

This home is of the Queen Anne style, featuring a turret and a Victorian wraparound porch. This two-story home features circular columns and is constructed of brick.

The home was built in 1896 by Ed Green, a local banker. According to local lore, Mr. Green served as a banker until 1926, at which time the bank fell. Upon close inspection of bank records, the inspectors believed that Mr. Green had embezzled from the bank. Mr. Green lost possession of the home at this time.

The home is located at 932 West Main and is presently owned by General and Mrs. William G. Moore.

White Chili

*This prize winner was a hit at a Harpeth Academy chili
cook-off. It is a great dish for a casual buffet.*

1 pound dried white beans
6 cups (or more) chicken broth
2 cloves of garlic, minced
2 medium onions, chopped
1 tablespoon vegetable oil
2 (4-ounce) cans chopped green chiles
2 teaspoons ground cumin
1¹/₂ teaspoons oregano
¹/₄ teaspoon ground cloves
¹/₄ teaspoon cayenne
4 cups chopped cooked chicken breasts
3 cups shredded Monterey Jack cheese

Sort the beans; rinse and drain. Combine the beans, broth, garlic
and half the onions in a large soup pot. Bring to a boil and reduce the heat.
Simmer, covered, for 3 hours or until the beans are very soft, adding
additional broth if necessary. Sauté the remaining onions in the vegetable
oil in a skillet until tender. Add the green chiles and seasonings and
mix well. Add the chicken. Stir the mixture into the bean mixture. Simmer
for 1 hour longer. Ladle into soup bowls and sprinkle with cheese.
For variety, provide an assortment of condiments such as salsa, chopped
green onions, sour cream, crumbled tortilla chips or guacamole
that can be added to suit individual tastes.
Yield: 8 to 10 servings.

Nana's Cajun Gumbo

1 large chicken, cut up
Salt, pepper and cayenne to taste
1/2 cup vegetable oil
1/2 cup all-purpose flour
1 large onion, finely chopped
1/2 cup finely chopped celery
1 cup finely chopped green bell pepper
2 cloves of garlic, pressed
1 bay leaf
3 tablespoons Worcestershire sauce
1 tablespoon Tabasco sauce
8 cups hot water
1 pound smoked sausage, sliced
1/2 cup minced green onions
1/2 cup minced parsley
2 tablespoons filé powder
5 cups hot cooked rice

Rinse the chicken and pat dry. Season the chicken with salt, pepper and cayenne. Brown the chicken on all sides in the oil in a large soup pot. Remove the chicken and set aside. Add the flour to the oil. Make a roux by cooking the flour in the oil until dark brown, stirring constantly. Add the onion to the roux. Cook until the onion is tender, stirring constantly. Add the chicken, celery, green pepper, garlic, bay leaf, Worcestershire sauce and Tabasco sauce. Cook until the vegetables are tender, stirring occasionally. Add the hot water gradually and mix well. Simmer, covered, for 1 hour, stirring frequently. Add the sausage and remove and discard the bay leaf. Simmer for 1 hour longer. Add the green onions and parsley. Simmer for 10 minutes. Remove from the heat. Add the filé powder and mix well. Ladle the gumbo over generous servings of hot cooked rice in large soup bowls. For variety, add desired amounts of fresh shrimp, oysters or crab meat with the green onions and parsley and simmer for 10 to 15 minutes.
Yield: 10 to 12 servings.

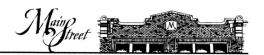

Chicken and Sausage Gumbo

$^3/_4$ cup all-purpose flour
8 ounces reduced-fat smoked sausage
6 (6-ounce) skinless chicken breasts
1 cup chopped onion
$^1/_2$ cup chopped green bell pepper
$^1/_2$ cup sliced celery
8 cups hot water
3 cloves of garlic, minced
2 bay leaves
2 teaspoons reduced-sodium Cajun seasoning
$^1/_2$ teaspoon thyme
1 tablespoon reduced-sodium Worcestershire sauce
1 teaspoon hot sauce
$^1/_2$ cup sliced green onions
4 cups hot cooked rice

Sprinkle the flour into a 9x13-inch baking pan. Bake at 400 degrees for 15 minutes or until dark golden brown, stirring every 5 minutes. Slice the sausage into $^1/_4$-inch slices. Spray a large heavy soup pot with nonstick cooking spray. Add the sausage. Cook over medium heat until brown, stirring frequently; drain the sausage and set aside. Spray the pot with additional nonstick cooking spray. Rinse the chicken and pat dry. Add the chicken to the pot. Cook until brown on all sides; drain the chicken and set aside. Spray the pot with nonstick cooking spray. Add the onion, green pepper and celery. Sauté until tender. Sprinkle with the browned flour. Stir in the water gradually and bring to a boil. Add the chicken, garlic, bay leaves, Cajun seasoning, thyme, Worcestershire sauce and hot sauce. Simmer, uncovered, for 1 hour. Remove the chicken and set aside to cool. Stir the sausage into the vegetable mixture. Simmer, uncovered, for 30 minutes. Add the green onions. Cook for 30 minutes longer. Debone the cooled chicken and cut into strips. Return the chicken to the gumbo. Heat to serving temperature. Discard the bay leaves. Serve the gumbo over the rice.
Yield: 6 to 8 servings.

*T*here was a public watering trough on the west side of the square. It was not uncommon to see a number of thirsty horses tied up there while their owners shopped and conducted business on Main Street.

Taco Soup

1½ pounds ground beef or ground turkey
1 large onion, chopped
2 (10-ounce) cans tomatoes with green chiles
1 (16-ounce) can kidney beans, drained
1 (16-ounce) can pinto beans
1 (16-ounce) can hominy, drained
1 envelope taco seasoning
1 envelope ranch salad dressing mix
Shredded Cheddar cheese (optional)
1 cup sour cream (optional)

Brown the ground beef with the onion in a soup pot, stirring frequently; drain. Add the tomatoes. Stir in the kidney beans, pinto beans and the hominy. Add the taco seasoning and salad dressing mix and mix well. Simmer for 2 hours or longer (or until you can't wait), adding 1 to 2 cups water if necessary to make soup of the desired consistency. Ladle into soup bowls. Garnish with shredded Cheddar cheese and a dollop of sour cream if desired.
Yield: 6 to 8 servings.

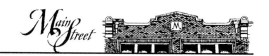

Kathy's Souper Easy Mexican Soup

1 (15-ounce) can stewed tomatoes
1 (10-ounce) can tomatoes with green chiles
1 (15-ounce) can whole kernel white corn
1 (10-ounce) can tomato soup
1 (10-ounce) can vegetable beef soup
1 (15-ounce) can chili with beans
Shredded Cheddar cheese
Sour cream
Corn chips

Combine the tomatoes, tomatoes with green chiles, corn, tomato soup, vegetable soup and chili in a large saucepan and mix well. Bring to a simmer over medium heat, stirring frequently. Layer desired amounts of cheese, sour cream and corn chips in individual soup bowls. Ladle the hot soup over the top.
Yield: 12 servings.

The D. T. Crockett store on the square sold groceries, hardware, and coal for heating. Next door was a blacksmith for shoeing horses and making tools, and a livery stable was located right around the corner.

Tortilla Soup

4 boneless skinless chicken breasts
2 (14-ounce) cans chicken broth
1 (4-ounce) can chopped green chiles
1 (10-ounce) can tomatoes and green chiles
1 medium onion, chopped
2 cloves of garlic, minced
1 tablespoon fresh lime juice
2 tablespoons minced fresh cilantro
$^1/_2$ teaspoon cayenne
$^1/_2$ teaspoon ground cumin
3 or 4 flour tortillas
Olive oil for frying
Shredded Monterey Jack cheese

Rinse the chicken. Cook the chicken in water to cover until tender;
drain and shred. Combine the chicken broth, green chiles,
tomatoes with green chiles, onion and garlic in a soup pot. Add the
shredded chicken. Bring to a simmer, stirring frequently. Simmer for 30 to
35 minutes. Add the lime juice, cilantro, cayenne and cumin. Simmer
for 10 to 15 minutes longer. Cut the tortillas into $^1/_2$x2-inch strips. Fry in
hot olive oil in a skillet until golden brown; drain on paper towels.
Ladle the soup into soup bowls. Garnish with shredded Monterey Jack
cheese and the tortilla strips. May thicken soup by adding the
desired amount of tomato paste to the soup or extend the recipe by
adding one 10-ounce can of tomato soup
Yield: 6 to 8 servings.

Minnesota Wild Rice Soup

This is a favorite at Merridee's Bread Basket on Fridays.

3 ounces uncooked wild rice
1 teaspoon vegetable oil
4 cups water
1 medium onion, chopped
6 tablespoons butter
10 tablespoons all-purpose flour
3 cups chicken stock
2 cups milk or half-and-half
Salt and pepper to taste

Sauté the wild rice in the oil in a large skillet until lightly toasted. Add the water. Simmer, covered, until the rice begins to pop open; do not overcook. Drain the rice, reserving 1 1/2 cups liquid. Set the rice and liquid aside. Sauté the onion in the butter in a soup pot over low heat until the onion is transparent. Add the flour and mix well. Cook over low heat for about 10 minutes, stirring occasionally; do not brown. Stir in the chicken stock and the reserved rice liquid gradually. Bring to a boil over medium heat, stirring constantly. Add the rice and milk. Cook over low heat for about 20 minutes, stirring frequently; do not allow soup to reach the boiling point. Season with salt and pepper. This soup may be prepared a day ahead, refrigerated and reheated.
Yield: 8 to 10 servings.

The original Tennessee-Alabama Railway Bridge over the Harpeth River was a covered bridge, as were several of the bridges in town during the early days.

There were several livery stables on Main Street, where horses were fed and stabled while their owners attended to business in town. When horseless carriages came to Franklin, many of these livery stables became automobile dealerships.

Spinach and Tortellini Soup

1 medium onion, finely chopped
1 clove of garlic, minced
$^1/_4$ cup margarine
9 cups chicken broth
2 (9-ounce) packages tortellini
2 teaspoons Italian seasoning
1 (28-ounce) can crushed tomatoes
10 to 12 ounces fresh spinach leaves

Sauté the onion and garlic in the margarine in a large soup pot until tender. Stir in the broth. Bring to a boil. Add the tortellini and cook until tender. Add the Italian seasoning and the crushed tomatoes. Heat to serving temperature. Rinse the spinach and discard stems. Tear the spinach into bite-size pieces. Add the spinach to the soup just before serving. Cook the soup just until the spinach is wilted. Serve immediately.
Yield: 8 to 10 servings.

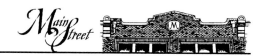

Potato-Mushroom Soup

4 cups chopped peeled potatoes
1 cup chopped onion
Salt to taste
4 cups water
1 (10-ounce) can cream of mushroom soup
$^1/_2$ cup sour cream
1 cup sliced mushrooms
1 teaspoon dillweed

Combine potatoes, onion, salt and water in a large saucepan.
Cook for 15 minutes or until the potatoes and onions are tender. Combine
the soup and sour cream in a bowl and beat until well mixed. Add a small
amount of the potato liquid to the soup mixture and beat until smooth.
Pour into the saucepan, mixing well. Add the mushrooms and dillweed.
Adjust the salt. Heat to serving temperature, stirring frequently.
Yield: 4 to 6 servings.

When Harpeth Ford
was located on Main Street,
gas pumps were located in
front of the building.
Motorists could pull right
over and fill up their cars.

Ham and Corn Chowder

This recipe was found stuck between the pages of an old English gardening book and it is a treasure.

2 medium potatoes, peeled, chopped
3 cups chicken broth
1 (16-ounce) can whole kernel corn
1 cup chopped celery
1/2 teaspoon hot pepper sauce
Salt and pepper to taste
2 tablespoons butter
3 tablespoons all-purpose flour
2 cups milk
1/2 cup shredded Cheddar cheese
1 cup chopped green pepper
2 cups chopped cooked ham

Combine the potatoes, chicken broth, corn, celery and hot pepper sauce in a soup pot. Add salt and pepper. Bring to a boil and reduce heat. Simmer, covered, for 30 minutes. Melt the butter in a heavy saucepan. Add the flour and blend well. Stir in the milk gradually. Cook until thickened, stirring constantly. Stir the mixture into the soup pot. Add the cheese, green pepper and ham and mix well. Cook, covered, over low heat until bubbly.
Yield: 8 to 10 servings.

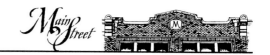
Shrimp Bisque

3 tablespoons all-purpose flour
2 teaspoons dried chopped parsley
3/4 teaspoon salt
1/4 teaspoon pepper
1/4 teaspoon garlic powder
1/4 teaspoon celery salt
1 small onion, grated
6 tablespoons butter
2 cups chicken broth
2 cups half-and-half or milk
12 ounces uncooked small shrimp, peeled, finely chopped

Combine the flour with the parsley, salt, pepper, garlic powder
and celery salt and set aside. Sauté the onion in butter in a soup pot over
medium-high heat for 5 minutes or until tender. Reduce the heat
to low and add the flour mixture, stirring constantly. Cook for several
minutes to make a roux, stirring constantly. Whisk in 1 cup of the broth.
Cook until smooth, whisking constantly. Whisk in the remaining broth and
half-and-half. Increase the heat to medium-high. Cook to the consistency
of heavy cream, whisking constantly. Add the shrimp. Cook over medium
heat for 4 to 5 minutes, stirring frequently. If the shrimp have been cooked,
add to the soup and heat just long enough to bring to serving temperature.
This recipe may prepared substituting lump crab meat for shrimp.
Yield: 4 to 6 servings.

*D*r. Hardin Perkins
Cochrane owned one of the
first horseless carriages in
Franklin. He often took a
carload of children out
to the Winstead Hills. At a
speed of 15 mph they
would coast down Columbia
Pike to town, laughing and
shrieking all the way.

Shrimp Chowder

$^1/_4$ cup chopped green onions
1 clove of garlic, minced
$^1/_4$ teaspoon cayenne
2 tablespoons butter
2 cups uncooked peeled small shrimp or frozen cooked shrimp
2 (10-ounce) cans cream of potato soup
3 ounces cream cheese, softened
$1^1/_2$ soup cans milk
1 (8-ounce) can whole kernel corn

Sauté the green onions, garlic and cayenne in the butter in a soup
pot until the green onions are about half cooked. Add the shrimp and cook
until the green onions are tender. Add the canned soup, cream cheese and
milk and mix well. Heat until well mixed, stirring frequently. Add the
undrained corn. Simmer, covered, for 10 minutes. If using frozen cooked
shrimp, add to the soup at the same time the corn is added.
Yield: 8 to 10 servings.

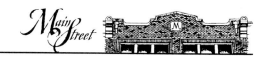

Brunswick Stew

1 (3-pound) chicken
2 ribs celery, cut into 1-inch pieces
1 onion, quartered
5 cups water
2 (10-ounce) packages frozen baby lima beans
2 (10-ounce) packages frozen whole kernel corn
1 cup chopped onion
2 (28-ounce) cans whole tomatoes
1 (8-ounce) can whole tomatoes
3 large potatoes, peeled, chopped
$^1/_2$ to 1 teaspoon red pepper
1 to 1$^1/_2$ teaspoons black pepper
2 cups water (optional)

Rinse the chicken. Combine the chicken, celery and quartered onion with 5 cups water in a soup pot. Bring to a boil and reduce the heat. Simmer, covered, for 1 hour or until the chicken is tender. Remove the chicken, celery and onion from the broth and set the broth aside. Discard the celery and onion. Skin, bone and chop the chicken. Add the chicken to the broth in the pot. Add the frozen vegetables and chopped onion. Drain the tomato liquid into the soup pot. Chop the tomatoes and add to the pot with the potatoes and seasonings. Bring to a boil and reduce the heat. Simmer, uncovered, for 3 hours or to the desired consistency, stirring frequently. May add the remaining 2 cups water as necessary.
Yield: 3$^1/_2$ quarts.

During the Battle of Franklin, the McEwen's old nanny refused to leave the dinner that she was cooking and seek refuge in the basement with the rest of the family. However, when a cannonball crashed into the kitchen and destroyed a large kettle she was using, the nanny wasted no time getting down the basement steps.

Chicken Stew

1 (2 to 3-pound) chicken, cut up
4 1/2 cups water
2 1/2 tablespoons chicken bouillon
1 cup chopped carrots
1 cup chopped celery
3/4 cup chopped onion
1 (8-ounce) jar mushrooms, drained
1 (8-ounce) package frozen sugar peas
1/2 cup small uncooked elbow macaroni

Rinse the chicken. Combine the chicken with the water and
bouillon in a soup pot. Bring to a boil and reduce the heat. Simmer,
covered, for 25 minutes or until chicken is tender. Remove the chicken
from the broth; bone and chop. Add the carrots, celery, onion and
mushrooms to the soup pot. Bring to a boil and reduce the heat. Simmer,
covered, until the vegetables are tender. Add the chicken and the sugar peas.
Simmer until heated through. Cook the macaroni using the package
directions; drain. Add the cooked macaroni to the soup pot just
before serving. Serve the stew with toasted French bread.
Yield: 5 servings.

Salads

Campbell-Westbrook House

Salads

Campbell-Westbrook House

In 1928 the Campbell-Westbrook home was constructed in the Hincheyville Historic District around an existing structure built in 1880. The weatherboard dwelling is a variation of the Queen Anne style that was popular during the late 1800s.

Brown Campbell built the house and resided there until 1910. Since that time the home as been rented as a single dwelling, redesigned and rented as apartments. In 1960 Eloise O'More rescued the home and with much renovation and loving care returned the home to its former grandeur. Miss O'More began the O'More School of Design in the home. As the school began to grow, a structure outside the home was used for classes and students used the upper bedrooms for boarding.

The home features original blue poplar floors and original doors with transoms that contain fire ruby glass. Upon entering the home visitors will find their eyes are drawn to the wood details of the grand staircase.

The home is located at 819 West Main Street, and the current owners are Mr. and Mrs. Larry Westbrook.

Apricot Salad

2 (3-ounce) packages apricot gelatin
$^2/3$ cup each sugar and water
2 (4-ounce) jars apricot baby food
1 (8-ounce) can crushed pineapple
8 ounces cream cheese, softened
1 (14-ounce) can sweetened condensed milk
$^1/2$ cup chopped nuts (optional)

Mix the gelatin, sugar and water in a large microwave-safe bowl. Microwave
on High until the mixture comes to a boil and gelatin and sugar dissolve,
stirring several times. Add the fruit and mix well. Set aside to cool. Beat the
cream cheese and condensed milk in a bowl until smooth and creamy. Add
to the gelatin mixture and mix well. Stir in the nuts. Pour into a 9-cup
mold. Chill until firm. Invert the mold onto a platter.
Yield: 12 servings.

Trella Garrison's Holiday Banana Salad

1 cup packed brown sugar
1 cup sugar
2 tablespoons all-purpose flour
3 tablespoons butter, softened
$^1/4$ cup vinegar
$^1/2$ cup water
2 eggs, beaten
Pinch of salt
6 large bananas, chopped

Mix the brown sugar, sugar and flour in a saucepan. Add the butter, vinegar,
water, eggs and salt and mix well. Cook over medium heat until smooth
and thickened, stirring constantly. Let stand at room temperature until cool.
Pour over the bananas in a bowl and mix gently. Serve immediately.
Yield: 8 to 12 servings.

For many years a school called the Franklin Female Institute was located at Five Points. Because the school administration did not want to use corporal punishment on the young ladies who were students there, rule-breakers were confined to their upstairs rooms and were not allowed to attend meals. These ingenious young ladies simply used rope to lower buckets to the ground, where they were filled with food by helpful friends.

Mimi's Fruit Salad

2 egg yolks
1/4 cup sugar
Juice of 2 lemons
1/8 teaspoon salt
1/4 cup cream
1 (15-ounce) can pineapple chunks
1 (11-ounce) can mandarin oranges
1 (21-ounce) can cherry pie filling
2 bananas, chopped
1/2 cup seedless grapes
2 cups whipping cream, whipped
2 cups miniature marshmallows

Beat the egg yolks in the top of a double boiler. Add the sugar, lemon juice, salt and cream; mix well. Cook over hot water until thick and creamy, stirring constantly. Set aside to cool then chill until serving time. Drain the pineapple and mandarin oranges. Combine the pineapple, mandarin oranges, pie filling, bananas and grapes in a serving bowl. Fold the whipped cream into the chilled dressing. Fold into the fruit mixture. Fold in the marshmallows. Serve immediately.
Yield: 12 to 15 servings.

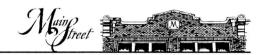

Make-Ahead Fruit Salad

1/2 cup mayonnaise
1/2 cup whipping cream, whipped
1 tablespoon lemon juice
2 cups drained peach slices
1/2 cup cherry halves
1 banana, sliced
1 cup crushed pineapple
1/4 cup chopped pecans
1 cup miniature marshmallows

Combine the mayonnaise, whipped cream and lemon juice in a large bowl.
Fold in the remaining ingredients. Chill until serving time.
Yield: 6 to 8 servings.

Miss Willie's Raspberry Salad

1 tablespoon unflavored gelatin (optional)
1 (3-ounce) package raspberry gelatin
1 cup boiling water
1 (10-ounce) package frozen raspberries
Juice of 1 small lemon
3 ounces cream cheese
1/4 to 1/2 cup finely chopped pecans

Soften the unflavored gelatin in a small amount of cold water. Dissolve the
raspberry gelatin in the boiling water in a bowl. Add the softened gelatin,
stirring until dissolved. Add the frozen raspberries and stir until the
raspberries are thawed. Stir in the lemon juice. Cut the cream cheese into 16
portions. Shape each portion into a small ball and roll in the pecans to coat.
Arrange the balls in a 1-quart mold. Spoon enough of the gelatin
mixture over the cream cheese balls to hold them in place. Chill until
set. Spoon the remaining gelatin mixture into the mold. Chill
until firm. Unmold the gelatin onto a serving platter.
Yield: 8 to 12 servings.

In 1899 the United Daughters of the Confederacy erected the Confederate Monument in the center of the square. As the granite Confederate infantryman was being hoisted into place, a horse and buggy became entangled in the ropes and the statue swung and hit the shaft of the monument. A large chip was broken from the soldier's hat. The statue was raised in spite of the damage.

Red and White Strawberry Salad

2 (3-ounce) packages strawberry gelatin
2 cups boiling water
2 (10-ounce) packages frozen strawberries, partially thawed
2 bananas, mashed
1 (20-ounce) can crushed pineapple, drained
Chopped nuts to taste
1 cup sour cream

Dissolve the gelatin in boiling water in a large bowl. Add the strawberries and stir until thawed. Add the bananas, pineapple and nuts; mix well. Pour half the mixture into a 9x13-inch dish. Chill until set. Chill the remaining gelatin mixture until thickened but of pouring consistency. Spread the congealed layer with sour cream. Spoon the partially congealed gelatin over the sour cream layer. Chill until firm. Cut the salad into squares and serve on a bed of crisp salad greens.
Yield: 12 to 15 servings.

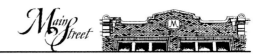

Patsy Anderson's Mexican Chicken Salad

1 pound boneless skinless chicken breasts
1 small onion, chopped
2 cups drained cooked kidney beans
3/4 cup olive oil
1/4 cup red wine vinegar
1 teaspoon sugar
1 tablespoon tomato paste
1 tablespoon chili powder
2 cloves of garlic, mashed
4 cups torn iceberg lettuce
2 cups torn romaine
1/2 cup chopped green onions
1 cup cherry tomatoes
Shredded Cheddar cheese to taste

Rinse the chicken. Cook the chicken in water to cover in a
saucepan until tender; drain, cool and chop. Combine the chicken,
chopped onion and kidney beans in a bowl. Combine the olive oil, vinegar,
sugar, tomato paste, chili powder and garlic in a jar, cover tightly and shake
vigorously to mix. Pour the desired amount of the marinade over the
chicken mixture and mix gently. Marinate, covered, in the refrigerator
overnight. Combine the lettuces and green onions in a salad bowl. Heat
the marinated chicken and bean mixture to serving temperature in a
saucepan over low heat. Spoon the hot mixture over the salad greens.
Top with the cherry tomatoes and shredded cheese.
Yield: 4 servings.

When Franklin's John Henry Eaton was in Washington serving as Secretary of State under President Andrew Jackson, he met and married a widow named Peggy O'Neal. The new Mrs. Eaton was not received by Washington society, so the Eatons decided to make their home in Franklin. The couple was met with a warm welcome and lived for many years in their home on Main Street.

Broccoli Salad

Florets of 1 bunch fresh broccoli
12 slices crisp-fried bacon, crumbled
1 cup golden raisins
$^{1}/_{2}$ cup chopped walnuts
$^{1}/_{4}$ to $^{1}/_{2}$ medium purple onion, chopped
2 cups cauliflowerets
1 cup mayonnaise
$^{1}/_{2}$ cup sugar
2 to 3 tablespoons white or apple cider vinegar
2 hard-boiled eggs, chopped
1 cup shredded Cheddar cheese

Combine the broccoli, bacon, raisins, walnuts, onion and cauliflower in a large salad bowl. Blend the mayonnaise, sugar and vinegar in a small bowl. Add to the broccoli mixture and toss to mix. Sprinkle the hard-boiled eggs and cheese over the top. Serve immediately. If salad is made ahead, do not add the bacon, onion and dressing until just before serving.
Yield: 6 servings.

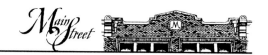

Caesar Salad

1 to 2 cloves of garlic, pressed
$^1/_4$ cup olive oil
3 or 4 drops of Worcestershire sauce
1 teaspoon prepared mustard
1 to 2 inches of anchovy paste
Salt and freshly ground pepper to taste
1 head romaine, torn
Juice of $^1/_2$ to 1 lemon
$^1/_4$ cup grated Parmesan cheese
Croutons

Combine the garlic, olive oil, Worcestershire sauce, mustard,
anchovy paste and salt and pepper in a large salad bowl; mix well. Add
the romaine. Sprinkle with the lemon juice and Parmesan
cheese and toss until romaine is coated with the dressing.
Add the croutons. Serve immediately.
Yield: 6 servings.

*I*n 1871 St. Phillips
Catholic Church was built
on the site of the old John
Eaton home. The bricks were
hand molded and fired
on the site, and heaven
directed Lancet windows were
incorporated into the design.

Sally Ewing Gaut, a colorful character who lived in the Maney house just off the square, made and flew the first Confederate flag in Franklin. During the war the Confederate Army used Mrs. Gaut and her family as a clearing house for clandestine information. The Gauts often climbed through a trapdoor onto their roof to watch the Union activities at nearby Fort Granger, and made trips through enemy lines to deliver information to the Confederates.

Chicory Salad

¹/2 cup olive oil
1¹/2 tablespoons light sesame oil
3 tablespoons red wine vinegar
3 cloves of garlic, minced
3 tablespoons soy sauce
¹/2 teaspoon Tabasco sauce
¹/2 teaspoon Szechwan pepper
¹/4 teaspoon muscovado sugar
6 to 8 cups chicory leaves

Combine the olive oil, sesame oil, vinegar, garlic, soy sauce, Tabasco sauce, pepper and sugar in a jar with a tightly fitting lid and shake vigorously to mix. Toss the desired amount of dressing with the chicory leaves in a salad bowl. Serve immediately.
Yield: 6 to 8 servings.

Tangy Coleslaw

8 cups shredded cabbage
$1/2$ red bell pepper, cut into strips
$1/2$ green bell pepper, cut into strips
$1/4$ red onion, cut into strips
1 carrot, shredded
2 tablespoons chopped fresh parsley
2 teaspoons grated lemon peel
Tangy Coleslaw Dressing (see below)

Combine the cabbage, peppers, onion, carrot, parsley and lemon peel in a large bowl, tossing to mix. Add the desired amount of Tangy Coleslaw Dressing and toss until vegetables are coated. Chill until serving time.
Yield: 8 servings.

Tangy Coleslaw Dressing

$1/2$ cup mayonnaise
$1/2$ cup sour cream
$1/4$ cup fresh lemon juice
2 tablespoons Dijon mustard
2 tablespoons olive oil
$2 1/4$ tablespoons sugar
$1/2$ teaspoon celery seeds
1 teaspoon pepper
1 tablespoon white wine vinegar
1 tablespoon prepared horseradish
$1 1/2$ teaspoons salt

Combine the mayonnaise, sour cream, lemon juice, mustard and olive oil in a bowl and whisk until well blended. Add the sugar, celery seeds, pepper, vinegar, horseradish and salt and mix well. Refrigerate, covered, until ready to use.

Mixed Greens with Rosemary Vinaigrette

1 head radicchio
2 heads frisée lettuce
6 heads mâche greens
2 bunches watercress
2 bunches arugula
Rosemary Vinaigrette (see below)
6 ounces mozzarella cheese, sliced
1 large ripe tomato, peeled, sliced

Rinse the greens and pat dry. Tear into bite-size pieces and
combine in a salad bowl. Add the desired amount of Rosemary
Vinaigrette and toss the greens to mix. Place mozzarella cheese slices
on the tomato slices and arrange over the greens. Serve immediately.
Yield: 4 to 6 servings.

Rosemary Vinaigrette

1 cup freshly snipped rosemary
3 shallots, chopped
1 cup rice vinegar
^{1}/4 cup corn oil
Juice of ^{1}/2 lemon
2 teaspoons white Worcestershire sauce

Combine the rosemary, shallots, vinegar, corn oil, lemon juice
and Worcestershire sauce in a bowl or jar with a tightly fitting lid and mix
well. Store any unused vinaigrette in the refrigerator.

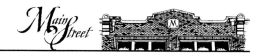

Ramen Salad

3 tablespoons sesame seeds
3 tablespoons sliced almonds
1 head iceberg lettuce, shredded
1 slice onion, separated into rings
Dressing for Ramen Salad (see below)
1 (3-ounce) package ramen noodles, crumbled

Sprinkle the sesame seeds and almonds in a single layer in a small
baking pan. Bake at 350 degrees for several minutes or until
toasted to a golden brown, stirring frequently. Combine the lettuce and
onion in a salad bowl. Add about half the Dressing for Ramen
Salad and toss to mix. Add the ramen noodles and the toasted sesame
seeds and almonds just before serving.
Yield: 4 to 6 servings.

Dressing for Ramen Salad

1 cup vegetable oil
$^3/_4$ cup white wine vinegar
$^1/_2$ cup sugar
1 teaspoon salt
1 teaspoon pepper
1 teaspoon MSG

Combine the vegetable oil, vinegar, sugar, salt, pepper and MSG
in a jar with a tightly fitting lid and shake vigorously.
Store in the refrigerator.

Dee Dorset's Spring Medley Salad

This is a wonderful salad to carry along for picnics and cookouts but elegant enough for Symphony on the Lawn at Carnton Mansion.

1 (16-ounce) can French-cut green beans
1 (15-ounce) can tender young green peas
1 (12-ounce) can Shoe Peg corn
1 (2-ounce) jar chopped pimento
1 cup finely chopped celery
1 cup finely chopped green bell pepper
1 cup finely chopped green onions
Sweet-and-Sour Marinade (see below)

Drain the canned vegetables well. Combine the canned vegetables in a large bowl. Add the chopped fresh vegetables. Add the hot Sweet-and-Sour Marinade and mix gently. Chill, covered, for several hours to overnight, stirring occasionally. Drain the salad before serving.
Yield: 12 to 15 servings.

Sweet-and-Sour Marinade

3/4 cup cider vinegar
1/2 cup vegetable oil
1 cup sugar
1 teaspoon salt
1 teaspoon pepper (optional)
1 tablespoon water

Combine the vinegar, oil, sugar, salt, pepper and water in a small saucepan. Cook over medium heat until the sugar dissolves, stirring frequently.

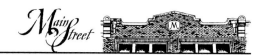

Tomato and Cucumber Salad

¹/₂ cup thinly sliced onion
2¹/₂ cups thinly sliced cucumbers
2 tablespoons finely chopped green bell pepper
2 tablespoons finely chopped red bell pepper
3 tablespoons white vinegar
¹/₂ teaspoon salt
1 teaspoon toasted cumin seeds
1¹/₂ cups cherry tomato halves
1 tablespoon finely chopped cilantro

Place the thinly sliced onion in a colander. Rinse under hot
running water for 1 to 2 minutes. Rinse with cold running water for
1 to 2 minutes. Drain well and pat the onion slices dry. (This
process will remove the strong oils and keep the onion slices white and
sweet.) Combine the onion slices with the cucumbers and bell peppers
in a bowl. Add the vinegar, salt and cumin seeds and toss to mix well.
Refrigerate, covered, for 1 hour or longer. Drain the vegetables well. Add
the tomatoes and cilantro and toss together. Serve immediately.
Yield: 6 servings.

When the Chickasaw
Indian delegation was in
Franklin to negotiate the
1830 treaty that led to their
removal from Tennessee, a
portrait painter at the
Marshall house painted a
portrait of one of the Native
Americans in his ceremonial
regalia. The subject was so
stunned when he saw the
portrait that he jumped out
the home's side window.

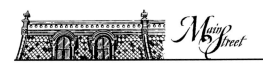

Kum Back Salad Dressing

1 cup mayonnaise
1/4 cup each chili sauce and catsup
1/2 cup vegetable oil
2 tablespoons water
2 cloves of garlic, grated
1 medium onion, grated
1 tablespoon Worcestershire sauce
Paprika, Tabasco sauce and salt to taste

Combine the first 5 ingredients in a bowl and blend well. Add the garlic, onion, Worcestershire sauce and seasonings and mix well. Store, covered, in the refrigerator for up to 2 weeks. Serve on any favorite salad.
Yield: 2 cups.

John Cosper's Thousand Island Salad Dressing

This dressing makes an especially good addition to chicken cacciatore.

1 cup mayonnaise
2 tablespoons chili sauce
1 tablespoon catsup
2 tablespoons minced olives
1 tablespoon chopped green bell pepper
1/2 to 1 tablespoon minced onion
1 hard-boiled egg, grated
Dash of Worcestershire sauce
Several drops each of vinegar and lemon juice
Salt to taste

Mix the mayonnaise, chili sauce and catsup in a small bowl. Add the olives, green pepper, onion and hard-boiled egg and mix well. Add the remaining ingredients. Chill, covered, until ready to serve.
Yield: 1 cup.

Entrées

LilliHouse

Entrées

Roast Beef Tenderloin
with Horseradish Sauce...67
Horseradish Sauce...67
Grilled Marinated Chuck Roast...68
Broiled Bacon-Wrapped Beef Patties...69
Nellie's Meat Loaf...69
Broccoli Beef Pie...70
Pizza Casserole...71
Citrus Pork Roast...72
Ginger and Garlic Pork...72
Pork Tenderloin with Wine Sauce...73
Marinated Pork Tenderloin...73
Chalupas...74
Glazed Spareribs...75
Papa's Rib and Chicken Marinade...76
Hank's Pennsylvania Barbecue Sauce...77
Baked Ham Loaf...77
Billy Reynolds' Baked Country Ham...78
Roast Leg of Lamb...79
Lamb Bundles...80
Grilled Veal Chops with Island Pepper
Rum Sauce...81
Marty Ligon's Chicken Cacciatore...82
Chicken Casserole with Broccoli...83
Spicy Chicken Casserole...84
Hot Chicken Enchiladas...85
Chicken Jerusalem...86
Steve Wariner's Chicken Mozzarella...87
Phyllo Chicken...88
Turkey Meat Loaf...89
Grilled Teriyaki Salmon...89
Baked Shrimp with Roasted Peppers
and Cheese...90
Grilled Swordfish...90

LilliHouse

This home is in the Hincheyville Historic District. The original lot owner was Patrick Darby. The house was built in 1894. It is believed to have been a wedding gift. The LilliHouse has a large bay window crowned by a turret covered with fish scale shingles. An interior wall of the home bears the following inscription in the plaster—"First Dinner Party April 10, 1895."

LilliHouse is the original James Lillie home. The Lillie family was very prominent in Franklin. James Lillie was a shipwright and bridge builder. He built the Lillie Mill which was operated in Franklin until it burned in the 1950s. Milton Lillie developed the first electric light system in Franklin, and Mrs. Pryor Lillie was a well-known teacher of Shakespearean drama, often staging plays on the front lawn of her home.

The current owner, Mrs. Marty Parrish Ligon, along with her husband Ronald, adorns this home with decorations for every holiday. Obviously, this home has been a favorite with children for many years. Located at 930 West Main Street, this home is a treat to see any time of the year.

Roast Beef Tenderloin with Horseradish Sauce

2 (3-pound) beef tenderloins
2 tablespoons crumbled dried rosemary
3 tablespoons cracked pepper
$^1/_4$ cup soy sauce
$^1/_4$ cup butter, softened
Horseradish Sauce (see below)

Rub the tenderloins with the rosemary and cracked pepper. Let the tenderloins stand at room temperature for 2 hours. Brush the tenderloins with soy sauce, rub with butter and place on a rack in a roasting pan. Preheat the oven to 500 degrees. Place the pan in the oven and reduce the temperature to 400 degrees. Roast for 40 minutes for rare. Let the tenderloins stand at room temperature until completely cooled. Wrap tightly and refrigerate until well chilled. Slice as desired and serve with Horseradish Sauce.
Yield: 12 servings.

Horseradish Sauce

1$^1/_2$ cups mayonnaise
1$^1/_2$ cups sour cream
$^1/_3$ cup chopped fresh chives
$^1/_4$ cup prepared horseradish
$^1/_4$ cup drained capers
1 tablespoon pepper

Combine the mayonnaise and sour cream in a bowl and blend well. Add the chives, horseradish, capers and pepper and mix well. Chill, covered, until serving time.

Many of the early homes in Franklin and Williamson County began life as a single pen log cabin. Later a second pen and dog trot porch were added. The third phase involved adding a second floor and covering the exterior logs with weatherboard. In the 1850s a Greek Revival porch was often added, and an Ell wing of additional rooms was sometimes attached to the rear of the home.

Grilled Marinated Chuck Roast

1 (2¹/2-pound) chuck roast, 2 inches thick
Unseasoned meat tenderizer
1 (5-ounce) bottle soy sauce
¹/4 cup packed brown sugar
1 tablespoon lemon juice
¹/4 cup bourbon
1 teaspoon Worcestershire sauce
1¹/2 cups water

Sprinkle the roast with the meat tenderizer using the package directions and pierce with a fork. Let the roast stand at room temperature for 1 hour. Combine the soy sauce, brown sugar, lemon juice, bourbon, Worcestershire sauce and water in a shallow dish and mix well. Add the roast, turning to coat all surfaces. Marinate, covered, in the refrigerator for 6 hours, turning once. Drain, reserving the marinade. Place the roast on the grill 5 inches above the hot coals. Grill for 30 minutes on each side or to desired degree of doneness, basting frequently with the reserved marinade.

Yield: 6 to 8 servings.

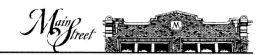

Broiled Bacon-Wrapped Beef Patties

2 pounds ground beef
1 cup shredded Cheddar cheese
$^2/_3$ cup chopped onion
$^1/_4$ cup catsup
2 tablespoons each Worcestershire sauce and Parmesan cheese
1 teaspoon salt
$^1/_4$ teaspoon pepper
2 eggs, beaten
12 slices bacon

Combine all ingredients except bacon and mix well. Shape into 2 logs.
Wrap 6 bacon slices around each; cut into patties between slices. Place the
patties on the rack in a broiler pan. Broil 7 inches from the heat source
for 6 minutes. Turn the patties over and broil for 3 minutes longer. May
bake unsliced bacon-wrapped logs at 375 degrees for 40 minutes.
Yield: 6 servings.

Nellie's Meat Loaf

1 (8-ounce) can crushed pineapple
1 cup catsup
2 tablespoons brown sugar
$1^1/_2$ pounds ground chuck
1 medium onion, chopped
4 slices bread, crumbled
Garlic powder, salt and pepper to taste
3 or 4 green bell pepper rings

Drain the pineapple, reserving 2 tablespoons juice. Mix the reserved juice,
catsup and brown sugar in a small bowl. Mix the ground chuck, onion,
bread, pineapple, seasonings and half the catsup mixture in a large bowl.
Shape into a loaf. Place in a 9x13-inch baking dish. Top with the pepper
rings and remaining catsup mixture. Bake at 350 degrees for 1 hour.
Yield: 6 to 8 servings.

*T*he eventual result was
a center hall structure with
one large room on each
side of the entry. This
style of home is often referred
to as "Tennessee Vernacular"
and is quite common in
the Franklin area.

Broccoli Beef Pie

*If there are any portions left over, freeze them
individually for later enjoyment.*

2 all ready pie pastries
1 pound lean ground beef
1 medium onion, chopped
1 clove of garlic, chopped
Salt and pepper to taste
1^1/$_4$ cups milk
3 ounces cream cheese, chopped
1 (10-ounce) package frozen chopped broccoli
1 extra large egg, beaten
^{3}/$_4$ cup shredded Monterey Jack cheese
^{3}/$_4$ cup shredded mozzarella cheese
Cayenne pepper to taste

Line a deep-dish pie plate with 1 of the pastries; trim and flute the edge.
Bake using package directions until golden brown. Cook the ground beef
with onion, garlic, salt and pepper in a large skillet until brown and crumbly, stirring frequently; drain well. Add the milk and cream cheese. Cook
until cream cheese melts, stirring constantly. Simmer for 10 minutes, stirring frequently. Cook the broccoli using the package directions and drain
well. Mix the broccoli with the egg and add to the ground beef mixture.
Spoon the ground beef mixture into the baked pie shell. Sprinkle the
Monterey Jack cheese and mozzarella cheese over the top. Cover with the
unbaked pie pastry. Press onto the baked pie shell and cut vents. Sprinkle
with cayenne. Bake at 350 degrees for 45 minutes. Serve hot.
Yield: 4 to 6 servings.

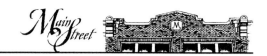

Pizza Casserole

1 (4-ounce) package sliced pepperoni
1 pound ground beef
1 medium onion, finely chopped
2 (8-ounce) cans tomato sauce
1 (4-ounce) can sliced mushrooms, drained, finely chopped
$^1/_2$ teaspoon dried basil
$^1/_2$ teaspoon dried oregano
1 (6-ounce) package spaghetti
3 tablespoons (scant) margarine
1 cup grated Parmesan cheese
8 ounces mozzarella cheese, shredded
8 ounces mozzarella cheese, sliced

Cover the pepperoni with water in a saucepan. Bring to a boil.
Boil for 5 minutes. Pour off the water and spread the pepperoni on paper
towels to complete draining. Cook the ground beef with onion in
a skillet until brown and crumbly, stirring frequently; drain well. Add the
tomato sauce, mushrooms, basil and oregano. Simmer for 10 minutes.
Cook the spaghetti using the package directions; drain well. Add the
margarine and toss the spaghetti until the margarine melts. Add the
Parmesan cheese and toss until mixed. Spread the spaghetti in a lightly
greased 9x13-inch baking dish. Add layers of the shredded mozzarella
cheese, pepperoni, ground beef mixture and sliced mozzarella cheese. Bake
at 350 degrees for 20 minutes; do not overbake. Let stand for several
minutes. Cut into squares and lift servings carefully from the pan
with a wide spatula. Serve with a tossed salad and French bread.
Yield: 8 servings.

The earliest homes in the
South employed an exterior
chimney that heated the
home adequately during the
mild southern winters but
did not overheat the rooms
when the fireplace was used
for cooking in the hot
summers. In contrast, early
homes in New England had
an interior chimney to
provide more heat during the
longer, more harsh winter.

One of Franklin's most lovely antebellum homes stood just behind the BGA campus. It was the home of the Bostic family and was the scene of many elegant parties. The home was called "Everbright" because its many windows were always shining with the light of candles.

Citrus Pork Roast

1 (4-pound) pork loin roast
1 clove of garlic, chopped
1 (1-inch) piece of gingerroot, chopped
1 cup orange marmalade
1/2 cup packed brown sugar
1/2 teaspoon nutmeg
1 cup orange marmalade
1/2 cup packed brown sugar
1 orange, sliced for garnish

Place the roast fat side up in a roasting pan. Roast, covered, at 325 degrees for 1 hour. Combine the next 5 ingredients in a blender. Process until smooth and pour into a small saucepan. Cook over low heat until bubbly, stirring constantly. Brush over the roast. Roast for 1 hour longer or to 175 degrees on a meat thermometer, brushing with the glaze several times. Remove the roast to a serving platter. Mix the remaining 1 cup marmalade and 1/2 cup brown sugar in a small bowl. Spoon over the roast before serving.
Yield: 8 servings.

Ginger and Garlic Pork

1/2 cup soy sauce
1/4 cup vegetable oil
3 tablespoons molasses
1 tablespoon ground ginger
2 teaspoons dry mustard
6 large cloves of garlic, minced
1 (5-pound) boneless, rolled pork loin roast

Whisk the first 6 ingredients in a bowl until well mixed. Place the roast in a shallow baking dish. Add the marinade. Refrigerate for 24 hours, turning occasionally. Drain, reserving the marinade. Place the roast in a roasting pan. Roast at 325 degrees for 2 hours, brushing frequently with marinade.
Yield: 10 to 15 servings.

Pork Tenderloin with Wine Sauce

4 (6-ounce) pork tenderloin medallions
Salt and pepper to taste
1 tablespoon olive oil
1 envelope gravy mix
1 cup red wine (preferably port)
2 tablespoons brandy
2 bay leaves
1 teaspoon crushed black peppercorns

Season the pork with salt and pepper. Heat the olive oil in a
large skillet. Add the pork. Cook for 6 to 8 minutes or until cooked
through, turning frequently. Prepare the gravy mix using the package
directions. Add the wine, brandy, bay leaves and peppercorns. Cook for 10
minutes longer, stirring frequently. Strain the sauce through a sieve. Place
the pork on a serving plate. Spoon the sauce over the top.
Yield: 4 servings.

Marinated Pork Tenderloin

1/3 cup fresh lime juice (3 large limes)
1/4 cup soy sauce
1 teaspoon dried oregano
1/2 teaspoon dried thyme
1 pound pork tenderloin
Salsa

Combine the lime juice, soy sauce, oregano and thyme in a sealable
plastic food storage bag. Add the tenderloin, turning to coat. Marinate in
the refrigerator for 24 hours. Drain, reserving the marinade. Grill the
tenderloin over hot coals until cooked through, turning and basting
frequently with the reserved marinade. Serve with lime wedges and salsa.
Yield: 2 to 4 servings.

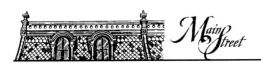

The Masonic Hall was built in 1923 and was the first three-story building in Tennessee. Federal troops who occupied the building during the Civil War left their autographs on an upstairs wall, where they remain today.

Chalupas

1 (3-pound) pork loin
1 pound dry pinto beans, sorted, rinsed
7 cups water
1 tablespoon salt
3 tablespoons chili powder
1 tablespoon ground cumin
1 tablespoon dried oregano
1 cup chopped onion
2 cloves of garlic, minced
2 (3-ounce) cans chopped green chiles
Black pepper to taste
Nacho chips
Shredded lettuce
Shredded Cheddar cheese
Chopped green onions
Chopped tomatoes
Sour cream
Taco sauce

Place the pork loin in a 3-quart Dutch oven. Add the beans, water, salt, chili powder, cumin, oregano, onion, garlic, green chiles and black pepper. Bring to a boil and reduce the heat. Simmer for 5 hours or until the pork falls from the bone. Shred the pork and discard the bone. Return the pork to the Dutch oven. Simmer for 1 hour longer. Spread a bed of nacho chips on the dinner plates. Ladle the pork mixture over the chips. Top with the lettuce, cheese, green onions, tomatoes, sour cream and taco sauce to taste.
Yield: 8 servings.

Glazed Spareribs

6 pounds pork spareribs
$^1/_2$ teaspoon salt
$^1/_2$ teaspoon pepper
Canned low-sodium chicken broth
1 (12-ounce) can frozen pineapple juice concentrate, thawed
1 tablespoon soy sauce
1 tablespoon Dijon mustard
2 teaspoons Tabasco sauce

Sprinkle the spareribs with salt and pepper. Wrap the ribs tightly
in foil and place on a baking sheet. Bake at 375 degrees for 1 hour and 20
minutes or until tender. Let the ribs stand, still wrapped in the foil,
at room temperature for 1 hour. Open the foil carefully and pour the
accumulated juices into a 2-cup measure. Add enough chicken broth to
measure $1^1/_3$ cups liquid. Pour into a heavy saucepan. Bring the
mixture to a boil. Boil for 10 minutes or until reduced to 1 cup liquid.
Blend the reduced juices with the pineapple juice concentrate in
a small bowl. Add the soy sauce, mustard and Tabasco sauce and mix well.
Grill the ribs over hot coals for 10 minutes on each side,
basting frequently with the pineapple juice mixture.
Yield: 4 to 8 servings.

In 1830 President Andrew
Jackson came here to
negotiate the removal of the
Chickasaw Indians from the
Tennessee area. The resulting
treaty, which was signed at
Masonic Hall, was the first in
a series of steps that led to
the Trail of Tears.

In 1842 a large comet passed over Franklin, causing considerable excitement. The next day a dusty yellow film settled over the town, frightening many residents who thought it was poisonous comet dust. In fact, it was only an unusually bad case of Middle Tennessee's pollen.

Papa's Rib and Chicken Marinade

1¹/₂ cups water
¹/₂ cup soy sauce
¹/₄ cup lemon juice
¹/₄ cup vegetable oil
2 teaspoons liquid smoke
2 cloves of garlic, pressed
¹/₂ teaspoon onion powder
¹/₂ teaspoon black pepper
2 teaspoons ground ginger
2 tablespoons brown sugar
Dash of Worcestershire sauce
Ribs or chicken
¹/₂ cup pure maple syrup

Combine the water, soy sauce, lemon juice, vegetable oil, liquid smoke, garlic, onion powder, black pepper, ground ginger, brown sugar and Worcestershire sauce in a bowl or sealable plastic food storage bag. Add the ribs or chicken and marinate in the refrigerator for 10 hours for ribs or 5 hours for chicken. Drain the ribs or chicken, reserving the marinade. Place the ribs or chicken bone side down on the grill rack over low coals. Cook for 25 minutes. Turn meat side down. Cook for 10 minutes. Mix 1¹/₄ cups of the reserved marinade with ¹/₂ cup pure maple syrup in a bowl. Cook for 10 minutes longer or until the ribs or chicken are cooked through, basting frequently with the maple syrup mixture. The marinade may be used twice before discarding but must be frozen between uses.
Yield: 2¹/₂ cups marinade.

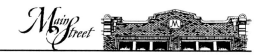

Hank's Pennsylvania Barbecue Sauce

1 cup catsup
1 tablespoon each peanut butter and prepared mustard
1 teaspoon pressed garlic
$^1/_2$ teaspoon pepper
1 teaspoon each oregano and chili powder
2 tablespoons brown sugar
1 medium onion, chopped
Ribs, chops or chicken

Mix the catsup and peanut butter in a small bowl. Add the mustard, garlic, pepper, oregano, chili powder and brown sugar and mix well. Stir in the onion. Place the ribs, chops or chicken on the grill over hot coals. Grill until cooked through, turning and basting frequently.
Yield: 1$^1/_2$ cups.

Baked Ham Loaf

2$^1/_2$ pounds ground baked ham
8 ounces bulk pork sausage
3 eggs, beaten
1 cup bread crumbs
1 cup milk
1 (8-ounce) can crushed pineapple
$^1/_4$ teaspoon pepper
1$^1/_2$ tablespoons prepared mustard
$^1/_2$ cup packed brown sugar

Combine the ham and sausage in a large bowl. Add the eggs, bread crumbs, milk, pineapple and pepper and mix well. Shape into a loaf in a shallow baking dish. Mix the mustard with the brown sugar in a small bowl. Spread the mixture over the ham loaf. Bake at 350 degrees for 1$^1/_2$ hours. For a moister loaf, baste the loaf with additional pineapple juice occasionally.
Yield: 8 servings.

During the 1830s a celebrated evangelist named Alexander Campbell came to Franklin to preach. It was a bitterly cold winter and Campbell spoke in several churches, but they either had no heat or the existing heat was so inadequate that the congregation was freezing in the sub-zero temperatures. Even though Campbell's sermons were powerfully delivered, no one in the frozen audiences responded to the great preacher's message.

Billy Reynolds' Baked Country Ham

You can depend on any ham prepared by this method—Billy even cures his own hams. This method works especially well if the baking stage starts about five o'clock in the afternoon so that after the last cooking time, the ham stays in the oven overnight.

1 country ham
2 quarts water
1 cup molasses

Soak the ham overnight in enough cold water to cover. Drain the ham and rinse well. Cut the hock from the ham. Place the ham skin side up in a large roaster. Add 2 quarts water and 1 cup molasses. Seal the roaster with a double layer of heavy-duty foil. Place the roaster in a preheated 500-degree oven. Bake for 30 minutes and turn off the oven. Let the roaster stand in the closed oven for 3 hours; do not open the oven. Turn the oven on to 500 degrees. Bake for 30 minutes longer. Turn off the oven. Let stand in the closed oven for 6 hours or longer; do not open the oven.

Yield: variable.

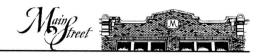

Marinated Roast Leg of Lamb

1 (6-pound) leg of lamb
5 large cloves of garlic, pressed
2 tablespoons mustard seeds
1 tablespoon dry mustard
1 tablespoon Dijon mustard
Dry mustard to taste
Salt and pepper to taste
1 (750-milliliter) bottle cabernet sauvignon
3 cups unsalted beef stock
1 (14-ounce) can reduced-sodium chicken broth
3 large shallots, finely chopped
Dry mustard to taste

Trim the leg of lamb and remove the large bone but let the shank bone remain. Combine the garlic, mustard seeds, 1 tablespoon dry mustard, Dijon mustard, salt and pepper in a bowl and mix to form a paste. Spread the paste over the surface of the lamb and wrap the lamb in plastic wrap. Chill in the refrigerator overnight. Combine the wine, beef stock, chicken broth and shallots in a large saucepan. Bring to a boil. Boil for 45 minutes or until reduced to about 1 cup. Preheat the oven to 375 degrees. Unwrap the lamb and place in a roasting pan. Sprinkle with additional dry mustard and salt and pepper to taste. Roast the lamb for $1^1/2$ hours or to 125 degrees on a meat thermometer. Remove the lamb to a serving platter. Add the reduced stock to the roasting pan. Bring to a boil over medium-high heat, stirring to deglaze the pan. Cook until reduced to the desired consistency, stirring frequently. Serve the sauce with the lamb.
Yield: 6 servings.

Lamb Bundles

Make as many bundles as needed. The ingredients listed are for just one.

1 carrot
1 onion
$^1/_2$ green bell pepper
$^1/_4$ cup uncooked long grain rice
1 lamb chop, 1 inch thick
$^1/_4$ teaspoon curry powder
$^3/_4$ cup tomato juice

Cut a 12-inch square of heavy-duty foil. Coat the foil with a small amount of vegetable oil. Cut the carrot crosswise then lengthwise into four portions. Slice the onion and cut the green pepper into $^1/_4$-inch strips. Mound the rice in the center of the foil. Place the lamb chop on the rice. Shape the foil around the rice and lamb chop as to form a cup. Place the vegetables on the lamb chop, sprinkle with curry powder and pour the tomato juice over the vegetables. Fold the foil over the top and seal tightly. Place the bundle in a 9x9-inch baking pan.
Bake at 350 degrees for $1^1/_2$ hours.
Yield: 1 serving.

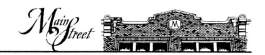

Grilled Veal Chops
with Island Pepper Rum Sauce

4 (8-ounce) veal loin chops
$^1/_2$ cup dark rum
$^1/_4$ cup olive oil
$^1/_3$ cup fresh lime juice (3 limes)
2 shallots, peeled, chopped
1 tablespoon chopped fresh thyme
1 teaspoon angostura bitters
$^1/_4$ cup honey
2 to 3 teaspoons Barbados pepper sauce or other thick hot sauce
6 tablespoons butter
Salt to taste

Arrange the veal chops in a single layer in a baking dish. Combine the rum, olive oil, lime juice, shallots, thyme, bitters, honey and pepper sauce in a bowl and whisk until well mixed. Pour the rum mixture over the veal chops. Let stand at room temperature for 1 hour or longer, turning once. Drain the veal chops, reserving the marinade. Grill the veal chops over hot coals until cooked through. Pour the marinade into a saucepan. Bring the marinade to a boil. Boil for 5 minutes. Cut the butter into small pieces. Add the butter to the hot marinade gradually, whisking constantly. Add the salt. Serve the sauce over the grilled veal chops.

Yield: 4 servings.

In 1839 Andrew Campbell was invited to become headmaster of Harpeth Academy, where the students had become rather unruly. Campbell decided to take control of the situation, bloodied a few noses, and restored order in the school.

Marty Ligon's Chicken Cacciatore

4 boneless skinless chicken breasts
1 medium onion, coarsely chopped
2 cloves of garlic, minced
1 teaspoon olive oil
2 carrots, thinly sliced
1 red, yellow or green bell pepper, cut into strips
1 (14-ounce) can Italian-flavored stewed tomatoes
$2/3$ cup chicken broth
2 teaspoons Worcestershire sauce
2 bay leaves
Pepper to taste
1 tablespoon cornstarch (optional)
3 tablespoons cold water (optional)
12 ounces angel hair pasta

Cut the chicken into strips and set aside. Sauté the onion and
garlic in olive oil in a large skillet until the onion is tender.
Add the carrots, bell pepper and undrained tomatoes. Cook, covered, over
medium heat for 3 minutes. Add the chicken, chicken broth,
Worcestershire sauce, bay leaves and pepper. Cook, covered, for 9
minutes, stirring occasionally. Reduce the heat to low. For thicker sauce,
add the cornstarch dissolved in the cold water. Cook until thickened,
stirring constantly. Remove the bay leaves. Cook the pasta using the package
directions. Serve the chicken mixture over the hot cooked pasta.
Yield: 4 servings.

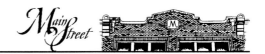

Chicken Casserole with Broccoli

1 (9-ounce) package frozen broccoli spears
$^1/_2$ cup mayonnaise
1 (10-ounce) can cream of mushroom soup
$^1/_2$ cup shredded Cheddar cheese
1 egg, beaten
2 cups chopped cooked chicken
Lemon pepper to taste
$^1/_2$ cup shredded Cheddar cheese
$^1/_2$ cup seasoned bread crumbs

Cook the broccoli using the package directions just until tender
and drain well. Arrange the broccoli spears in a 9x9-inch baking pan
sprayed with nonstick cooking spray. Combine the mayonnaise,
soup, $^1/_2$ cup cheese and egg in a bowl and mix well. Stir in the chicken and
lemon pepper. Spoon the chicken mixture over the broccoli. Sprinkle
the remaining $^1/_2$ cup cheese over the chicken mixture and top with the
bread crumbs. Bake at 350 degrees for 15 minutes or until heated
through. May substitute steamed fresh broccoli or cooked fresh or
frozen asparagus spears for the frozen broccoli.
Yield: 4 servings.

By 1836 life in Franklin
had become much more
comfortable than it had
been for the early pioneers
who founded the town. Some
residents were leading a
rather luxurious lifestyle.
Tappan and Co., a store
on the square, capitalized on
that lifestyle by stocking an
inventory that included four
baskets of fine Champagne.

During the early years the mortality rate for women and children was very high. Many widowers buried their wives in the city cemetery and ordered elaborate tombstones engraved with long flowery epitaphs. Often the lonely widower had remarried before the stonecutter had finished his memorial to the first wife.

Spicy Chicken Casserole

Serve this tasty chicken over a bed of Mexican rice.

4 boneless skinless chicken breasts
2 teaspoons vegetable oil
1/2 cup thinly sliced onion
1/2 medium green bell pepper, cut into strips
1 cup whole kernel corn
1 (8-ounce) can tomato sauce
1 tablespoon minced fresh cilantro
1 teaspoon chili powder
3 tablespoons chili sauce
1/2 to 1 cup shredded Monterey Jack cheese with jalapeños

Rinse the chicken and pat dry. Cut the chicken into strips. Sauté the chicken in hot oil in a skillet for 3 to 5 minutes. Add the onion and green pepper. Sauté for 5 minutes longer. Combine the corn, tomato sauce, cilantro, chili powder and chili sauce in a bowl and mix well. Add the cheese and the chicken mixture; mix well. Spoon into a lightly greased 1 1/2-quart baking dish. Bake, covered, at 350 degrees for 30 minutes.
Yield: 4 to 6 servings.

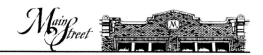

Hot Chicken Enchiladas

Please note the title of this recipe—hot it is. For those with milder tastes, be sure to reduce the amount of chiles.

2 pounds chicken breasts
3 cups chicken broth
1/3 cup all-purpose flour
1 (16-ounce) can tomatoes
3 green chiles, chopped
1/2 cup chopped onion
1 clove of garlic, minced
1 teaspoon sugar
1 teaspoon ground cumin
1/2 teaspoon basil
1/2 teaspoon oregano
Salt and pepper to taste
1 pound (about) Monterey Jack cheese
12 flour or corn tortillas
3/4 cup sour cream

Rinse the chicken and pat dry. Cook the chicken breasts as desired. Bone, cut into strips and set aside. Blend the broth with flour in a saucepan. Cook over medium heat until thickened, stirring constantly. Add the undrained tomatoes, chiles, onion, garlic, sugar, cumin, basil, oregano, salt and pepper. Bring to a simmer, stirring constantly and remove from the heat. Cut a portion of the cheese into 12 strips and shred the remaining cheese. Place a strip of cheese and some chicken on each tortilla, roll to enclose the filling and arrange seam side down in a greased large baking dish. Blend the sour cream into the tomato mixture. Spoon the mixture over the enchiladas Sprinkle with the shredded cheese. Bake at 400 degrees for 15 minutes or until the cheese melts.
Yield: 12 enchiladas.

Francis Asbury, the organizer of the United Methodist Church, came to Franklin in 1812. For 45 years Asbury rode the circuit through pioneer America, preaching and starting churches at a salary of $80 per month.

Chicken Jerusalem

8 boneless skinless chicken breasts
1 cup all-purpose flour
1 teaspoon garlic salt
1 teaspoon dried dillweed
¼ cup vegetable oil
2 tablespoons butter
2 tablespoons flour
2 to 3 cups half-and-half
1 tablespoon Dijon mustard
1 (16-ounce) can artichoke hearts, drained, quartered

Rinse the chicken and pat dry. Mix 1 cup flour with garlic salt and dillweed. Coat the chicken with the seasoned flour. Fry the chicken in hot oil in a large skillet for about 15 minutes or until light brown and cooked through. Remove the chicken to a serving platter; keep warm. Pour off the oil, leaving the crusty brown particles. Add the butter to the skillet. Sprinkle 2 tablespoons flour into the skillet. Cook over medium heat, stirring constantly. Add enough of the half-and-half gradually to make a sauce the consistency of pancake batter, stirring constantly. Blend in the mustard. Add the artichoke hearts. Heat to serving temperature. Spoon over the chicken. Serve with hot cooked rice.
Yield: 8 servings.

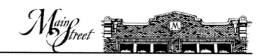

Steve Wariner's Chicken Mozzarella

2 cups cooked spaghetti (do not add oil or salt during cooking)
1 pound boneless skinless chicken breasts
$3/4$ cup tomato sauce
1 cup thinly sliced fresh mushrooms
$1/4$ cup thinly sliced green bell pepper
$1/4$ cup finely chopped yellow onion
$1/4$ teaspoon garlic powder
$1/4$ teaspoon dried basil leaves
$1/2$ teaspoon dried oregano leaves
$1/4$ teaspoon freshly ground black pepper
$1/8$ teaspoon fennel seeds
$1/2$ teaspoon reduced-sodium Worcestershire sauce
2 tablespoons chopped fresh parsley
1 to 2 tablespoons dry red wine
$1/2$ cup shredded mozzarella cheese
1 tablespoon freshly grated Parmesan cheese

Rinse the cooked spaghetti with cold water and drain well. Place the spaghetti in a layer in an 8-inch square baking dish sprayed with nonstick cooking spray. Pound the chicken breasts to flatten to a $1/4$-inch thickness and cut into bite-size pieces. Arrange the chicken over the spaghetti. Combine the tomato sauce with mushrooms, green pepper, onion, garlic powder, basil, oregano, pepper, fennel seeds, Worcestershire sauce, parsley and wine and mix well. Spoon the sauce over the chicken and spaghetti. Bake, uncovered, at 350 degrees for 30 minutes. Sprinkle with the mozzarella cheese. Bake for 8 to 10 minutes longer or until the cheese melts. Sprinkle with the Parmesan cheese. To freeze, layer the spaghetti, chicken and sauce in a foil baking pan, wrap tightly in heavy-duty foil and store in the freezer for up to a month. When ready to use, let thaw completely in the refrigerator, then bake, still wrapped, at 350 degrees for 40 to 45 minutes. Unwrap, top with the mozzarella cheese and bake for 8 to 10 minutes longer. Sprinkle with the Parmesan cheese before serving.
Yield: 4 servings.

Phyllo Chicken

8 ounces bacon
1 (10-ounce) package frozen chopped broccoli, thawed
6 green onions, finely chopped
3 cups chopped cooked chicken
2 cups shredded Swiss cheese
6 eggs
1 cup evaporated milk
1/2 cup milk
Salt and pepper to taste
1/2 cup melted butter
12 sheets phyllo dough

Fry the bacon in a skillet until crisp; drain and crumble. Drain the
broccoli well. Combine the bacon, broccoli, green onions,
chicken and cheese in a large bowl and toss to mix well. Whisk the eggs
in a medium bowl. Add the evaporated milk, milk, salt and pepper and
whisk until well blended. Brush the bottom and sides of a 9x13-inch
baking dish with a portion of the butter. Alternate layers of 6 sheets of
phyllo with some of the remaining butter in the baking dish. Keep
the unused phyllo covered to prevent drying. Spoon the chicken mixture
into the prepared baking dish. Pour the egg mixture over the chicken
mixture. Cover with alternate layers of the remaining phyllo and butter,
ending with butter. Bake at 375 degrees for 35 to 40 minutes or
until a knife inserted near the center comes out clean.
Yield: 8 to 10 servings.

Turkey Meat Loaf

3 pounds ground fresh turkey
$1/4$ cup seasoned bread crumbs
$1/3$ cup milk
1 onion, chopped
$1/4$ cup catsup
$1/2$ teaspoon poultry seasoning
$1/4$ teaspoon basil leaves
Salt and pepper to taste
$1/4$ cup catsup
1 tablespoon light brown sugar
$1/4$ teaspoon nutmeg
1 teaspoon dry mustard

Combine the first 9 ingredients in a bowl and mix well. Shape
into a loaf in a 9x13-inch baking dish. Bake at 350 degrees for 40
minutes. Spoon mixture of $1/4$ cup catsup and remaining ingredients
over the loaf. Bake for 20 to 30 minutes longer.
Yield: 8 servings.

Grilled Teriyaki Salmon

1 cup soy sauce
Juice of 1 lemon
$1/4$ cup each dry sherry and chopped green onions
2 tablespoons minced fresh gingerroot
1 clove of garlic, minced
1 tablespoon freshly ground pepper
Pinch of cayenne pepper
4 salmon fillets

Mix the first 8 ingredients in a shallow dish. Add the salmon, turning
to coat. Marinate, covered, in the refrigerator for 5 hours; drain. Grill the
salmon over hot coals for 5 to 7 minutes on each side.
Yield: 4 servings.

Roasted Peppers

This method works well for both bell and chile peppers. Select large smooth peppers if possible. Rinse well. Place in a single layer on a grill or broiler pan. Grill or broil until the skin blisters and blackens, turning as necessary. Alternatively, you may place peppers on a baking sheet and bake at 475 to 500 degrees until the skin blisters, turning as necessary. Place hot peppers in a metal bowl or pan and cover with dampened paper towels. Let stand to steam until cool enough to handle. Pierce the skin at the edge of the cap. The skin will peel off as easily as slipping off a glove. Freeze the peppers, peeled or unpeeled, in appropriate portions in sealable plastic bags. When ready to use, make a slit from cap to tip and remove the seeds and membranes.

Baked Shrimp with Roasted Peppers and Cheese

3/4 cup olive oil
1/2 cup butter
3 white onions, sliced
5 each red and green bell peppers, roasted
2 pounds medium shrimp, peeled, deveined
1/2 teaspoon salt
1/4 teaspoon pepper
8 ounces each Muenster and Monterey Jack cheese, shredded

Heat the olive oil and butter in a skillet over medium heat. Add the onions. Sauté until the onions are brown. Peel and seed the peppers and cut into strips. Add to the skillet. Cook over low heat for 15 minutes, stirring occasionally. Add the shrimp and seasonings. Cook for 5 minutes. Adjust the seasonings. Spoon into a large casserole. Sprinkle with the cheeses. Bake at 325 degrees for 20 minutes or until the cheeses have melted.
Yield: 6 servings.

Grilled Swordfish

4 swordfish steaks, 1 inch thick
2 tablespoons each Dijon mustard and fresh lime juice
1/2 cup olive oil
2 shallots, chopped
2 tablespoons each chopped fresh rosemary and pepper

Arrange the swordfish steaks in a shallow glass dish. Blend the mustard and lime juice in a small bowl. Whisk in the olive oil gradually. Add the shallots, rosemary and pepper and mix well. Pour over the swordfish, turning to coat. Marinate, covered, in the refrigerator for 3 hours; drain. Grill over hot coals for 5 minutes on each side or until the swordfish flakes easily.
Yield: 4 servings.

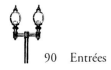

Brunch

Long-Babbitt House

Brunch

King Crab Salad Pie...93
Pastry Shell...93
Breakfast Casserole...94
Elegant Egg Casserole...94
Morning Strata...95
Sausage and Apple Brunch Pie...96
Crunchy Breakfast Pie...96
Savory Cheese and Onion Pie...97
Swiss and Crab Meat Quiche...97
Sausage and Mushroom Casserole...98
Spicy Sausage Turnovers...99
Stuffed Breakfast Pita...100
Autumn Apple Bake...100
Garlic Cheese Grits...101
Apple Crescent Coffee Cake...101
Apricot Almond Coffee Cake...102
Almond Cream Cheese Rolls...103
Apricot-Filled Crepes...104
Apricot Jam...105
Apple Flaps...105
Marilyn Lehew's Overnight
French Toast...106

Long-Babbitt House

The Long-Babbitt House was constructed in 1831. It is one of the oldest dwellings in the Hincheyville Historic District. Its distinctive "Y" shape makes it one of the most unique homes in Franklin. A small spring-fed stream referred to as "Town Creek" runs near this home. It is hardly as noticeable now as it was when a stone bridge marked its passage over West Main Street.

One of the earliest references to the Long-Babbitt House is the deed of sale which records the transfer of the lot in 1832 from Thomas Dudley to Judith Long. The property was sold to Mr. Weems for $1,552 in 1851. Tradition has it that the Haynes family added the brick wings. This addition is probably over one hundred years old, since they disposed of the property in 1890.

Entering from the front door of the home, a room is located on either side. A hall extends to the back forming the bottom of the "Y." All the other rooms, including the kitchen, are in the older section of the home.

This beautiful home is located at 805 West Main Street, and is owned by Mrs. Mary Frances Ligon.

King Crab Salad Pie

1 (7-ounce) can king crab meat
3 hard-cooked eggs, chopped
$^1/_2$ cup chopped celery
2 tablespoons minced green onions
1 cup shredded Cheddar cheese
1 cup mayonnaise
1 (10-ounce) package frozen chopped broccoli or asparagus
Pastry Shell (see below)

Drain and slice the crab meat. Combine with the hard-cooked
eggs, celery, green onions and cheese in a bowl. Add the mayonnaise
and mix gently. Cook the broccoli and drain well. Spoon the broccoli
evenly over the Pastry Shell. Spoon the crab meat mixture over
the broccoli. Bake at 375 degrees for 30 minutes or until golden
brown. Serve warm or chilled. Cut into wedges.
Yield: 6 servings.

Pastry Shell

$1^1/_4$ cups all-purpose flour
2 teaspoons baking powder
$^1/_2$ teaspoon salt
$^1/_2$ cup butter, softened
$^1/_4$ cup milk
1 tablespoon freeze-dried or frozen chopped chives

Sift the flour, baking powder and salt into a bowl.
Cut in the butter until crumbly. Add the milk and chives and mix
until the mixture forms a ball. Press over the bottom and
up side of a deep-dish 9-inch pie plate.

A Confederate soldier once left his army to go and visit his family who lived near Franklin. The Union soldiers in the area learned of his whereabouts and went in the dead of night to arrest him. When they knocked on the door of the soldier's farmhouse, his wife told him to hide under the feather mattress on their bed, then tucked their small children into the bed on top of the mattress.

Breakfast Casserole

3 cups French bread cubes
3 cups chopped cooked ham
8 ounces Cheddar cheese, shredded
1 (4-ounce) can sliced mushrooms, drained
8 eggs
3 cups milk
3 tablespoons all-purpose flour
1/2 to 1 tablespoon dry mustard
3 tablespoons melted butter

Combine the first 4 ingredients in a large bowl and toss to mix. Spread in a 10x15-inch baking pan. Beat the eggs in a medium bowl. Add the milk, flour, dry mustard and butter and beat until well blended. Pour over the ham mixture. Refrigerate, covered, overnight. Bake, uncovered, at 325 degrees for 1 hour and 10 minutes or until golden brown.
Yield: 10 to 12 servings.

Elegant Egg Casserole

16 ounces Monterey Jack cheese, shredded
1 (4-ounce) can chopped green chiles, drained
32 ounces small curd cottage cheese
1 cup all-purpose flour
1 teaspoon baking powder
1/2 cup melted butter
10 eggs, beaten

Combine the Monterey Jack cheese, green chiles and cottage cheese in a large bowl and mix well. Add the flour mixed with baking powder, butter and eggs; mix well. Pour into a greased 9x13-inch baking dish. Bake at 400 degrees for 15 minutes. Reduce the oven temperature to 350 degrees. Bake for 30 minutes longer or until golden brown.
Yield: 12 to 15 servings.

Morning Strata

1 pound lite sausage
8 eggs
3 cups skim milk
10 slices bread, cubed
2 cups shredded low-fat Cheddar cheese
2 cups sliced fresh mushrooms
2 tablespoons melted margarine
2 tablespoons all-purpose flour
1 tablespoon dry mustard
2 teaspoons basil
1 teaspoon salt (optional)
1 (9-ounce) package frozen asparagus, thawed

Cook the sausage in a large skillet until brown and crumbly,
stirring frequently; drain well. Beat the eggs in a large bowl. Add the
skim milk and beat until well blended. Add the bread, cheese, mushrooms
and margarine; mix well. Mix the flour, dry mustard, basil and salt together
and stir into the egg mixture. Drain and chop the asparagus. Stir into the
egg mixture. Pour into a greased 9x13-inch baking dish or 2 greased pie
plates. Refrigerate, covered, overnight. Bake at 350 degrees for 60 to
70 minutes for the 9x13-inch baking dish or for 50 to 60 minutes
for the pie plates. The strata may be frozen and thawed
in the refrigerator overnight before baking.
Yield: 8 to 10 servings.

The Union soldiers
searched the house to no
avail, even failing to
notice that the woman had
slipped on her husband's
shoes instead of her own
when she jumped hastily
from the bed. Thanks to
his wife's ingenuity, the
Confederate escaped capture.

Sausage and Apple Brunch Pie

1 unbaked (9-inch) pie shell
1 pound pork sausage links
1 (21-ounce) can apple pie filling
1 cup shredded Cheddar cheese
1/2 cup packed brown sugar

Bake the pie shell at 375 degrees for 10 minutes. Cook the sausage links
in a skillet until brown; drain on paper towels. Pour the pie filling
into the partially baked pie shell. Arrange the sausage links spoke-fashion on
the pie filling. Sprinkle with the cheese and top with the brown sugar.
Bake at 375 degrees for 25 to 35 minutes.
Yield: 6 to 8 servings.

Crunchy Breakfast Pie

4 slices bacon
2 cups frozen hashed brown potatoes with onions and peppers
6 eggs
1/4 cup milk
1/2 teaspoon salt
1/8 teaspoon pepper
1 cup shredded Cheddar cheese

Arrange the bacon in a microwave-safe pie plate. Microwave the bacon,
loosely covered with paper towels, until crisp. Drain the bacon on
paper towels, reserving the drippings in the pie plate. Layer the hashed
browns in the drippings in the pie plate. Microwave, uncovered,
for 7 minutes. Beat the eggs with milk, salt and pepper until well blended.
Pour over the potatoes. Microwave, covered with plastic wrap, for 7
minutes, turning every 3 minutes. Sprinkle with the cheese and crumble
the bacon over the top. Microwave, covered, for 2 minutes. Let stand
for 5 minutes before cutting into wedges.
Yield: 6 servings.

Savory Cheese and Onion Pie

10 ounces Gruyère cheese, shredded
2 tablespoons all-purpose flour
2 large onions, sliced
2 tablespoons butter
1 unbaked (9- or 10-inch) pie shell
2 large tomatoes, sliced
1 teaspoon dried basil
2 eggs, beaten
$^3/_4$ cup whipping cream or half-and-half

Toss the cheese with the flour; set aside. Sauté the onions in butter
until tender; remove with a slotted spoon. Layer $^1/_3$ of the cheese and
sautéed onions in the pie shell. Heat tomatoes and basil in the skillet
for 2 minutes. Arrange over the onions. Cover with the remaining cheese.
Pour a mixture of eggs and whipping cream over the top. Bake
at 350 degrees for 35 minutes or until set.
Yield: 6 servings.

Swiss and Crab Meat Quiche

1 cup shredded Swiss cheese
1 (6-ounce) can crab meat, drained
2 green onions with tops, sliced
1 unbaked (9-inch) pie shell
4 eggs, beaten
1 cup whipping cream
$^1/_2$ teaspoon each grated lemon peel, salt and dry mustard
$^1/_4$ teaspoon ground mace
$^1/_4$ cup sliced almonds

Layer the cheese, crab meat and green onions in the pie shell. Pour
a mixture of the next 6 ingredients over the layers. Top with the almonds.
Bake at 325 degrees for 45 minutes or until set.
Yield: 6 servings.

During the 1930s there was a popular series of children's books called Those Plummer Children. The stories were based on the lives of a large Franklin family.

Sausage and Mushroom Casserole

Complete the brunch menu with a baked fruit dish and garlic cheese grits.

2 pounds hot bulk pork sausage
$2^1/4$ cups seasoned croutons
4 eggs, beaten
$2^1/4$ cups milk
1 (10-ounce) can cream of mushroom soup
1 (8-ounce) can sliced mushrooms, drained
$3/4$ teaspoon dry mustard
Pepper and garlic powder to taste
2 cups shredded Cheddar cheese
Cherry tomato halves
Chopped fresh parsley

Cook the sausage in a large skillet until brown and crumbly, stirring frequently; drain well. Layer the croutons and cooked sausage in a greased 2-quart baking dish. Combine the eggs, milk and soup in a bowl and mix well. Stir in the mushrooms, dry mustard, pepper and garlic powder. Pour over the sausage. Refrigerate, covered, overnight. Bake, uncovered, at 325 degrees for 55 minutes. Sprinkle the cheese over the top. Bake for 5 minutes longer or until the cheese melts. Arrange the tomato halves over the top and sprinkle with parsley.
Yield: 8 servings.

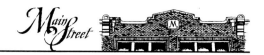

Spicy Sausage Turnovers

4 ounces ground fresh turkey
4 ounces bulk pork sausage
$1/2$ teaspoon onion salt
1 tablespoon all-purpose flour
1 tablespoon cooking wine
1 package all ready pie pastries
1 egg yolk
1 tablespoon water
Paprika to taste

Cook the turkey and sausage in a skillet until brown and crumbly, stirring frequently; drain. Add the onion salt, flour and wine and mix well; set aside. Unfold the pie pastries and roll to $1/8$-inch thickness on a lightly floured surface. Cut into 3-inch rounds with a cookie cutter. Spoon a small amount of the sausage mixture onto half of each circle and moisten the edges with a small amount of water. Fold the pastry over the sausage mixture and press the edges with a fork to seal and enclose the filling. Place the turnovers on an ungreased baking sheet. Beat the egg yolk with 1 tablespoon water. Brush over the turnovers. Cut 2 small slits in the top of each turnover. Bake at 400 degrees for 12 to 14 minutes or until golden brown. Sprinkle with paprika. Serve hot. May freeze and reheat at 350 degrees for 8 minutes.
Yield: 2 to 3 dozen.

Stuffed Breakfast Pita

2 (6-inch) whole wheat pita rounds
1 tablespoon each chopped onion and green bell pepper
$^1/_2$ cup chopped cooked lean ham
2 eggs, beaten
$^1/_2$ cup shredded low-fat Swiss cheese
8 tomato slices

Cut the pita rounds into halves crosswise and wrap in foil. Bake at
350 degrees for 5 minutes. Add the onion and green pepper to a
preheated skillet sprayed with nonstick cooking spray. Sauté over medium-
high heat until tender. Add the ham, eggs and cheese. Cook until eggs
are firm, stirring constantly. Fill each pita half with 2 tomato slices and
about $^1/_4$ cup of the egg mixture. Serve immediately.
Yield: 4 servings.

Autumn Apple Bake

3 cups chopped peeled green apples
1 (12-ounce) package cranberries
2 tablespoons all-purpose flour
1 cup sugar
$^1/_2$ teaspoon cinnamon (optional)
$^1/_2$ cup packed dark brown sugar
$^1/_2$ cup all-purpose flour
$^1/_4$ teaspoon cinnamon (optional)
$^1/_2$ cup margarine
$^3/_4$ cup chopped pecans

Toss the apples and cranberries with a mixture of the next 3 ingredients.
Spread in a greased 9x13-inch baking dish. Mix the brown sugar, $^1/_2$ cup
flour and $^1/_4$ teaspoon cinnamon in a bowl. Cut in the margarine until
crumbly. Add the pecans. Spoon over apple mixture. Bake at 325 degrees
for 30 to 40 minutes or until apples are tender and top is golden brown.
Yield: 6 servings.

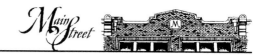

Garlic Cheese Grits

1 cup uncooked grits
1 tablespoon salt
4 cups boiling water
$^1/_2$ cup (scant) margarine
1 (6-ounce) roll garlic cheese
8 ounces sharp Cheddar cheese, shredded
2 tablespoons Worcestershire sauce
Paprika to taste

Cook the grits with salt in the boiling water in a large saucepan using the package directions. Add the margarine, garlic cheese, Cheddar cheese and Worcestershire sauce. Cook until melted, stirring constantly. Pour into a greased 9x13-inch baking dish. Sprinkle with paprika. Bake at 350 degrees for 20 minutes.
Yield: 8 to 10 servings.

Apple Crescent Coffee Cake

2 (8-count) cans crescent rolls
1 (14-ounce) package coconut-pecan frosting mix
2 cups chopped peeled tart apples
$^1/_4$ cup melted butter
$^1/_4$ cup plus 1 tablespoon orange juice
$^1/_2$ cup confectioners' sugar

Unroll dough. Line an ungreased 9x13-inch baking dish with half the dough, sealing the perforations. Sprinkle with 1 cup of the frosting mix. Layer the apples over the frosting mix. Drizzle half the butter over the top. Press the remaining dough into a rectangle and seal the perforations. Place over the apple layer. Mix the remaining butter, remaining frosting mix and $^1/_4$ cup orange juice in a bowl. Spread over the dough. Bake at 375 degrees for 25 minutes or until golden brown. Drizzle with a mixture of the confectioners' sugar and 1 tablespoon orange juice.
Yield: 12 servings.

In 1918 a terrible flu epidemic struck the town, and large public gatherings were forbidden. The members of Fourth Avenue Church of Christ did not wish to cancel their worship services, so they met on the church steps in the freezing cold for hymns, prayer and the Lord's Supper.

Like most homes and churches in Franklin, the McEwen House on Main Street was full of wounded soldiers for several weeks following the Battle of Franklin.

Apricot Almond Coffee Cake

1 cup butter, softened
2 cups sugar
2 eggs
1 teaspoon almond extract
2 cups all-purpose flour
1 teaspoon baking powder
1/4 teaspoon salt
1 cup sour cream
1 cup sliced almonds
1 (10-ounce) jar apricot preserves

Beat the butter at medium speed in a mixer bowl for 2 minutes or until creamy. Add the sugar gradually, beating constantly. Beat for 5 to 7 minutes. Add the eggs 1 at a time and beat just until yellow disappears. Blend in the almond extract. Mix the flour, baking powder and salt together. Add to the butter mixture alternately with the sour cream beginning and ending with the flour mixture; beat at low speed just until blended after each addition. Pour about 1/3 of the batter into a greased and floured 12-cup bundt pan. Sprinkle with half the almonds and dot with spoonfuls of half the preserves. Spoon the remaining batter into the pan and top with the remaining almonds and preserves. Bake at 350 degrees for 50 to 55 minutes or until a wooden pick inserted near the center comes out clean. Cool in the pan on a wire rack for 10 to 15 minutes. Invert the coffee cake onto the wire rack to cool completely. May substitute vanilla extract for the almond extract, pecans for the almonds and a mixture of 3 tablespoons brown sugar and 2 teaspoons ground cinnamon for the apricot preserves.
Yield: 12 servings.

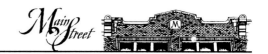

Almond Cream Cheese Rolls

8 ounces cream cheese, softened
1 teaspoon almond extract
$^1/_2$ cup confectioners' sugar
$^1/_2$ cup sliced almonds
2 (8-count) cans crescent rolls
$^2/_3$ cup confectioners' sugar
$^1/_2$ teaspoon almond extract
3 to 4 teaspoons milk

Combine the cream cheese, 1 teaspoon almond extract and $^1/_2$ cup confectioners' sugar in a bowl and beat until light and fluffy; set aside. Crumble the almonds into small pieces; set aside. Set the cream cheese mixture and the almonds aside. Open one can of the rolls and shape into an 8x14-inch rectangle, pressing the edges and perforations to seal. Spread the dough with half the cream cheese mixture and sprinkle with half the almonds. Roll as for a jelly roll from a long side and pinch the edge to seal. Slice into 10 to 12 rolls and arrange cut side down on an ungreased baking sheet. Repeat with the remaining roll dough, cream cheese mixture and almonds. Sprinkle the rolls with additional almonds if desired. Bake at 350 degrees for 17 to 23 minutes or until golden brown. Combine $^2/_3$ cup confectioners' sugar, $^1/_2$ teaspoon almond extract and enough milk to make glaze of desired consistency. Drizzle the glaze over the warm rolls and serve immediately.
Yield: 2 dozen.

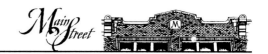

When the Federal troops returned to collect their wounded comrades, they gave each of the McEwen daughters a United States five dollar bill—a small fortune to most southerners at that time.

Apricot-Filled Crepes

*Although the name is French, the origin is German.
Crepes are a common German breakfast food imported into
this region by German immigrants.*

3 eggs
1 cup all-purpose flour
1 cup milk
1 tablespoon vegetable oil
Apricot Jam (see page 105)

Combine the eggs, flour, milk and 1 tablespoon vegetable oil in a
blender container. Process for 1 minute. Scrape the sides of the container
with a rubber spatula and process for 15 seconds longer. Refrigerate the
batter for 1 hour to allow the flour particles to swell and soften so that the
crepes will be light in texture. Brush a 10- or 12-inch skillet with a
small amount of additional vegetable oil. Place the skillet over medium heat
and preheat until the oil is hot but not smoking. Pour $1/2$ cup of the
batter into the skillet and tilt the pan in all directions to flow over the
bottom of the skillet in a thin film. Cook for about 1 minute. Lift the edge
of the crepe to test for doneness. The crepe is ready to flip when it can be
shaken loose from the pan. Flip the crepe over and cook for about
30 seconds longer (this side is rarely more than spotty brown.) Place the
crepe on a tile to cool. Repeat with the remaining batter. Stack the
crepes between layers of waxed paper to prevent sticking. Spoon a small
amount of the Apricot Jam onto each crepe and roll up to enclose the
filling. Serve warm. Crepes may also be filled with
sausage, cheese, jelly or other favorite fillings.
Yield: 8 crepes.

Apricot Jam

1 (6-ounce) package dried apricots
2 cups sugar
$1/2$ ($13/4$-ounce) package Sure-Jel

Place the apricots in a 1-quart microwave-safe bowl. Cover generously with water. Let stand for 4 to 6 hours to overnight. Add the sugar and Sure-Jel and mix well. Microwave on High for 5 minutes. Mash the apricots. Microwave for 3 minutes. Stir and mash the apricots. Let stand until cool.
Yield: 2 cups.

Apple Flaps

$11/2$ cups all-purpose flour
2 tablespoons sugar
1 tablespoon baking powder
$1/4$ teaspoon salt
2 eggs
$3/4$ cup milk
2 tablespoons melted butter
1 cup applesauce

Sift the flour, sugar, baking powder and salt together into a bowl. Beat the eggs with milk in a mixer bowl. Add the butter and applesauce and blend well. Add the applesauce mixture to the flour mixture; mix just until moistened. Pour 2 tablespoons of the batter at a time onto a hot lightly greased griddle. Bake until light brown on both sides, turning once.
Yield: 20 pancakes.

*I*ndustrialization came to Franklin in the late nineteenth and early twentieth centuries. Many of the small cottages on Franklin's side streets were built as housing for the growing number of workers in the new industries.

Marilyn Lehew's Overnight French Toast

1/4 cup butter, softened
12 (3/4-inch-thick) slices French bread
6 eggs
1 1/2 cups milk
1/4 cup sugar
2 tablespoons maple syrup
1 teaspoon vanilla extract
1/2 teaspoon salt
Confectioners' sugar to taste

Spread the butter over the bottom and sides of a large shallow baking pan.
Arrange the bread slices in a single layer in the pan. Beat the eggs in a bowl.
Add the milk, sugar, maple syrup, vanilla and salt and beat until well
blended. Pour over the bread slices, turning the bread to coat. Refrigerate,
covered, overnight. Bake the French toast, uncovered, at 400 degrees for 10
minutes. Turn the slices over. Bake for 3 to 4 minutes longer. Remove the
slices to a serving plate. Sprinkle with confectioners' sugar. Serve with maple
syrup with English walnuts or pecan pieces added.
Yield: 6 servings.

Pasta

Harris-McEwen-Merrit House

Pasta

Harris-McEwen-Merrit House

This elaborate Italianate structure is part of the Hincheyville Historic District. It was constructed in two phases—a one-story brick section in 1832 and the current impressive structure in 1849.

The original owner was John B. McEwen. Daughter, Frances McEwen, while a student at the Franklin Female Institute, is quoted with this memory of the tumultuous days leading up to the Battle of Franklin, "The bell called us to chapel. We were told to take our books and go home, as there was every indication that we would be in the midst of battle that day." The McEwens' four daughters hid in the basement during the Battle of Franklin, then emerged to spend many weeks feeding and tending to wounded soldiers. The McEwens' only son had died as a teenager, and Mr. McEwen made a habit of taking in worthy young men and educating them, giving them a head start on successful lives and careers. Mr. McEwen was an early real estate developer, owning the popular resort at Fernvale and starting Franklin's first subdivision, McEwen's addition to Hincheyville.

The Harris-McEwen-Merrit home is located at 612 Fair Street. This historical home is meticulously maintained by its current owners, Mr. and Mrs. Greg Daily.

Susan's Pasta Salad

The dressing is what makes this salad wonderful. Although the dressing ingredients are many, they are usually on hand in our pantries.

1¹/2 cups fresh snow peas
4 cups fresh broccoli florets
2¹/2 cups cherry tomatoes, cut into halves
2 cups sliced fresh mushrooms
1 (6-ounce) can sliced black olives, drained
16 ounces cheese-stuffed tortellini
¹/2 cup sliced green onions
¹/3 cup red wine vinegar
¹/3 cup vegetable oil
¹/3 cup olive oil
2 tablespoons chopped fresh parsley
2 cloves of garlic, minced
2 teaspoons dried basil
1 teaspoon dried dillweed
1 teaspoon salt
¹/2 teaspoon pepper
¹/2 teaspoon sugar
¹/2 teaspoon oregano
1¹/2 teaspoons Dijon mustard

Combine the snow peas, broccoli, tomatoes, mushrooms and olives in a large bowl and mix well. Cook the pasta using the package directions. Drain the pasta and let cool. Combine the green onions, vinegar, vegetable oil, olive oil, parsley, garlic, basil, dillweed, salt, pepper, sugar, oregano and Dijon mustard in a bowl, whisking until mixed. Toss with the pasta and vegetables. Chill for 1 to 2 hours. May substitute 8 ounces cheese-stuffed tortellini and 8 ounces bow-tie or other pasta for the 16 ounces cheese-stuffed tortellini.
Yield: 6 to 8 servings.

Before fast food and drive-in windows came to Franklin, several pie wagons operated on Main Street. One of the best known was Chapman's, which was a fixture on the square from 1922 until 1946. In addition to its delicious meals, Chapman's was known for the window boxes of beautiful flowers that graced its exterior.

Chicken and Mango Chutney Salad

The dressing for this chicken salad is so delicious you'll want to eat it with a spoon.

1/2 cup mango chutney
1 cup sour cream
1/4 cup mayonnaise
1 1/2 teaspoons freshly grated ginger
1 tablespoon honey
1/2 teaspoon salt
1 teaspoon curry powder, or to taste
12 ounces rotelle or fusilli
2 cups shredded cooked chicken
2/3 cup thinly sliced celery
1 cup seedless red grapes, cut into halves
1/4 cup chopped green bell pepper
3/4 cup toasted slivered almonds

Combine the chutney, sour cream, mayonnaise, ginger, honey, salt and curry powder in a medium bowl and mix well. Set aside; do not refrigerate. Cook the pasta using the package directions until al dente. Drain, rinse with cold water and drain again. Mix the pasta, chicken and 1 cup of the dressing in a large bowl. Let stand to allow the flavors to blend. Add the celery, grapes, green pepper and 1/2 cup of the almonds and mix well. Chill until 30 minutes before serving. Spoon the remaining dressing over the salad. Garnish with the remaining 1/4 cup almonds and additional red grapes. May substitute other types of chutney for the mango chutney.
Yield: 6 servings.

Mary's Pasta Chicken Salad

16 ounces fettuccini, cooked, drained
1 cup Italian salad dressing
6 cups chopped cooked chicken
2 cups chopped artichoke hearts
2 cups light mayonnaise
2 tablespoons chopped parsley
1 cup chopped green onions
2 teaspoons each oregano and basil

Combine the fettuccini with the Italian salad dressing in a large bowl.
Marinate in the refrigerator for 6 to 8 hours. Add the chicken,
artichoke hearts, mayonnaise, parsley, green onions, oregano and basil and
mix well. Marinate in the refrigerator for 8 to 10 hours.
Garnish with avocado and tomato slices.
Yield: 8 servings.

Chicken with Angel Hair Pasta

1 cup ranch salad dressing
^{1}/$_3$ cup Dijonnaise
4 whole chicken breasts
^{1}/$_2$ cup butter
^{1}/$_3$ cup white cooking wine
10 ounces angel hair pasta, cooked, drained
Chopped parsley (optional)

Whisk the salad dressing and Dijonnaise in a small bowl and set aside.
Pound the chicken flat. Sauté the chicken in the butter in a skillet until
browned and cooked through. Remove to a dish and keep warm. Pour the
wine into the skillet. Cook over medium-high heat for 5 minutes, deglazing
the skillet. Whisk in the dressing mixture. Layer the pasta and chicken in a
9x12-inch dish. Pour the wine sauce over the top. Sprinkle with the parsley.
Yield: 6 to 8 servings.

Grilled Chicken with Pasta and Peppers

$1/2$ cup chopped onion
1 each red, green and yellow bell peppers, cut into strips
3 tablespoons olive oil
4 boneless skinless chicken breasts, grilled, chopped
8 ounces fettuccini, cooked, drained
Freshly ground pepper and Parmesan cheese to taste

Sauté the onion and bell peppers in the olive oil in a skillet just until
tender. Add the chicken. Cook until heated through, stirring constantly.
Spoon over the pasta on serving plates. Sprinkle with the pepper and cheese.
Yield: 4 to 6 servings.

Fettuccini with Ham and Peas

2 teaspoons minced garlic
$1/2$ tablespoon margarine
8 ounces thinly sliced ham, cooked
1 cup frozen green peas, thawed
12 to 16 ounces fettuccini
$1/2$ cup margarine
1 cup grated Parmesan cheese
1 cup sour cream
Pepper to taste

Sauté the garlic in $1/2$ tablespoon margarine in a large skillet
over medium heat. Add the ham and peas. Sauté for 3 to 5 minutes
or until heated through. Remove from the heat and keep warm.
Cook the fettuccini using the package directions, omitting the salt. Drain
well and return to the pan. Add $1/2$ cup margarine, stirring until melted.
Add the cheese and sour cream and mix well. Add the ham mixture, stirring
to toss gently. Season with the pepper. Serve immediately.
Yield: 6 servings.

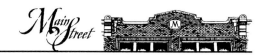

Green and White Lasagna

8 lasagna noodles
1 cup finely chopped onion
1 cup finely chopped celery
2 cloves of garlic, minced
1 tablespoon vegetable oil
2 tablespoons all-purpose flour
2 teaspoons dried basil, crushed
2 teaspoons dried oregano, crushed
$3/4$ teaspoon salt
$1/2$ teaspoon pepper
2 (10-ounce) packages frozen cut broccoli, thawed
1 cup light cream or milk
3 cups shredded Gouda cheese
3 ounces cream cheese, cut into $1/2$-inch cubes
$1/2$ cup dry white wine
$1^1/2$ cups cream-style cottage cheese
1 egg, slightly beaten
8 ounces mozzarella cheese, sliced or shredded
$1/4$ cup grated Parmesan cheese

Cook the lasagna using the package directions; drain and set aside.
Cook the onion, celery and garlic in the oil in a large skillet until tender but
not browned. Stir in the flour, basil, oregano, salt and pepper. Add
the broccoli and cream. Cook until thickened and bubbly, stirring
constantly. Cook for 1 to 2 minutes longer, stirring constantly. Add the
Gouda cheese and cream cheese. Cook over low heat until the
cheeses are melted, stirring constantly. Stir in the wine and remove from
the heat. Mix the cottage cheese with the egg in a bowl. Layer the
noodles, broccoli mixture, cottage cheese mixture, mozzarella cheese and
Parmesan cheese $1/2$ at a time in a greased 9x13-inch baking dish.
Bake at 375 degrees for 30 to 35 minutes or until heated
through. Let stand for 10 minutes.
Yield: 12 servings.

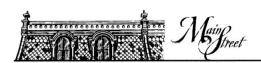

The Franklin Rotary Club
Rodeo, which began in 1949,
became the largest rodeo east
of the Mississippi River.

Fettuccini with Pesto Sauce

*This is a basic génoese pesto that Italians use in sauces,
soups, omelets and anything else that they can think of. It is so
easy, but it's my most requested recipe!*

2 cups firmly packed fresh basil leaves
1/2 cup olive oil
2 tablespoons pine nuts
2 cloves of garlic, peeled
1 teaspoon salt, or to taste
1/2 cup grated Parmesan cheese
2 tablespoons grated Romano cheese
3 tablespoons butter, softened
12 ounces fettuccini
2 tablespoons hot water

Combine the basil leaves, olive oil, pine nuts, garlic and salt in a blender
container. Process until mixed and pour into a bowl. Beat in the cheeses by
hand. Beat in the butter. Cook the fettuccini using the package directions.
Drain and return to the pan. Toss with the pesto and hot water. Serve
immediately. The pesto will keep for several weeks in the refrigerator. If
freezing the pesto, omit the cheese and butter and add them after thawing.
The pesto may be served with boursin cheese or tomatoes as an appetizer or
whisked with balsamic vinegar and olive oil for a salad dressing.
Yield: 6 servings.

Linguini with My Special Shrimp Creation

10 sun-dried tomatoes
3 tablespoons white wine or water
5 slices prosciutto, chopped,
1 medium onion, chopped
4 to 6 cloves of garlic, chopped
1 medium green bell pepper, chopped
1/2 cup white wine
1 1/2 cups chicken broth
5 to 10 fresh basil leaves, chopped
20 medium shrimp, peeled, deveined
Salt and pepper to taste
1 1/2 pounds linguini, cooked, drained
Grated Romano cheese

Cut the tomatoes with scissors. Combine with 3 tablespoons
wine in a small saucepan. Cook over medium heat until the tomatoes are
softened. Brown the prosciutto in a medium saucepan over
medium heat. Combine the tomatoes and ham in a bowl and set aside.
Sauté the onion and garlic in a large nonstick skillet. Add the green pepper.
Cook until the green pepper begins to soften. Add 1/2 cup wine
and the chicken broth. Simmer over medium heat for 15 minutes. Stir in
the basil. Reduce heat to low. Add the shrimp. Simmer for 5 minutes. Add
the tomato mixture. Season with the salt and pepper. Simmer for 5 minutes.
Arrange the linguini on serving plates. Top with the sauce. Sprinkle with
the cheese. Serve with a salad and French or Italian bread.
Yield: 4 servings.

From 1907 to 1941 the Interurban Railway made hourly trips between the square in Franklin and the courthouse square in Nashville. Many Franklin residents used this convenient service to commute to work in Nashville or to go into the city for shopping. Fare was ten cents and the train often stopped along the way to pick up passengers who stood alongside the tracks.

Springtime Pasta

The sauce cooks quickly and is ready to serve in minutes, so be sure to prepare all the vegetables before starting to cook.

1/2 cup butter
8 ounces asparagus, cut into 1-inch spears
8 ounces mushrooms, sliced
1/4 cup slivered prosciutto or ham
1 medium carrot, thinly sliced
1 medium zucchini, chopped
3 green onions, sliced
1/2 cup frozen tiny peas, thawed
1 teaspoon dried basil
1/2 teaspoon salt
1/8 teaspoon nutmeg, or to taste
1/8 teaspoon white pepper, or to taste
1 cup whipping cream
8 ounces angel hair pasta, cooked, drained
1/2 cup freshly grated Parmesan cheese
Chopped fresh parsley

Melt the butter in a large skillet over medium-high heat. Add the asparagus, mushrooms, prosciutto, carrot and zucchini. Cook for 3 minutes, stirring occasionally. Cover and cook for 1 minute. Add the green onions, peas, basil, salt, nutmeg, white pepper and whipping cream and mix well. Increase the heat to high. Cook until the liquid comes to a full boil. Pour the vegetable sauce over the pasta in a large serving bowl and toss to mix well. Add half the cheese and toss well. Sprinkle with the parsley and remaining cheese.
Yield: 4 to 6 servings.

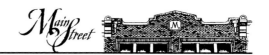

Zucchini Vermicelli Casserole

1 large rib celery, chopped
3 green onions, chopped
1 small green bell pepper, chopped
$1/4$ cup olive oil
3 medium tomatoes, peeled, chopped
4 medium zucchini, sliced into $1/8$-inch-thick rounds
Seasoned salt and pepper to taste
Garlic powder to taste
$1/2$ teaspoon oregano
$1/2$ teaspoon basil
5 ounces vermicelli, broken into small pieces
$1/4$ cup (or more) grated Parmesan cheese

Sauté the celery, green onions and green pepper in the olive oil in
a skillet. Add the tomatoes and zucchini. Season with the seasoned salt,
pepper, garlic powder, oregano and basil. Cook, covered, until the
vegetables are wilted, stirring occasionally. Cook the pasta using the package
directions until al dente and drain well. Combine with the zucchini
mixture and mix well. Stir in the cheese. Pour into a 2-quart casserole. Bake
at 325 degrees for 30 minutes or until bubbly and heated through.
Garnish with additional cheese. May substitute a 1-pound
can of tomatoes for the fresh tomatoes.
Yield: 6 to 8 servings.

On the corner of the
square and Third Avenue
North is the old Interurban
station, with its covered
porches to keep waiting
passengers dry in wet weather
and shaded in the summer.

Citrus Rice

4 cups hot cooked rice
2 teaspoons grated lime or lemon zest
4 teaspoons lime or lemon juice
1 tablespoon chopped parsley
$^1/_8$ teaspoon salt, or to taste
1 tablespoon olive oil

Combine the rice, lime zest, lime juice, parsley, salt and olive oil
in a bowl and mix well. Serve immediately.
Yield: 4 servings.

Pecan Pilaf

3 tablespoons margarine
1 cup chopped pecans
5 tablespoons margarine
$^1/_2$ cup chopped onion
2 cups long grain brown rice
3 (14-ounce) cans chicken broth
$^3/_4$ to 1 cup water
1 teaspoon salt
$^1/_4$ teaspoon thyme
$^1/_8$ teaspoon pepper
2 tablespoons chopped parsley

Melt 3 tablespoons margarine in a large skillet. Add the pecans. Sauté
for 10 minutes or until browned; do not overcook. Remove the pecans and
wipe the skillet clean. Melt 5 tablespoons margarine in the skillet. Add
the onion. Sauté for 3 minutes. Add the rice and stir until the rice and
onion are coated. Add the broth, water, salt, thyme and pepper
and mix well. Simmer, covered, for 45 minutes or until tender. Remove
from the heat and stir in the pecans and parsley.
Yield: 4 servings.

Breads

Mapledene

Breads

Mapledene

Mapledene was constructed in 1880 by George W. Smithson. It is part of the Hincheyville Historic District. It is quite an imposing brick home, given the fact that it was built during the hard times that the South endured following the Civil War. It is noted for its enclosed sunroom and massive entry posts.

George Smithson was married to Sally M. Henderson, who was the daughter of Dr. Samuel Henderson. It is believed that this home was a wedding gift. Mr. Smithson was from the Peytonsville community. After being wounded in the Battle of Franklin he returned to civilian life and, in 1865, opened Smithson & Kennedy Dry Goods Store on Main Street.

Mapledene is located at 908 West Main Street. It is currently owned by Marcia E. Williams and David G. Ogilvie.

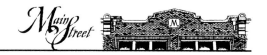

Angel Biscuits

This dough will keep for up to 2 weeks in the refrigerator if placed in a greased bowl and tightly covered. Or, you may cut out the biscuits and freeze them in plastic bags until ready to use. Thaw for 20 to 30 minutes before baking. Angel biscuits do not need to rise before baking.

2 envelopes dry yeast
$^1/_2$ cup lukewarm water
5 cups all-purpose flour
1 teaspoon baking soda
3 tablespoons sugar
1 teaspoon salt
1 tablespoon baking powder
$^3/_4$ cup shortening
2 cups buttermilk

Dissolve the yeast in lukewarm water in a small bowl. Sift the flour, baking soda, sugar, salt and baking powder into a large bowl. Cut in the shortening until mixture is crumbly. Add yeast and buttermilk, stirring with a large spoon until the mixture is moistened. Roll out on a floured board to $^1/_2$-inch thickness. Cut with a biscuit cutter. Place on a baking sheet. Bake at 400 degrees for 20 minutes or until lightly browned.

Yield: 5 dozen.

Three-Grain Biscuits

1$\frac{1}{3}$ cups all-purpose flour
$\frac{1}{3}$ cup yellow stone-ground cornmeal
$\frac{1}{3}$ cup rolled oats
1 teaspoon each baking powder and baking soda
$\frac{1}{2}$ teaspoon salt
$\frac{1}{4}$ cup butter, cut into small pieces
$\frac{1}{2}$ cup each sour cream and milk

Combine the flour, cornmeal, oats, baking powder, baking soda and
salt in a mixer bowl. Cut in the butter until mixture is crumbly. Blend the
sour cream and milk in a small bowl. Add to the dry ingredients, stirring
until moistened. Turn the dough onto a floured surface. Knead 10 to 12
times, adding additional flour if necessary to prevent sticking. Pat the
dough to $\frac{3}{4}$-inch thickness. Cut into 2-inch circles. Place on a greased
baking sheet. Bake at 350 degrees for 15 minutes.
Yield: 14 biscuits.

Parmesan Crescents

2 cups all-purpose flour
2 cups cottage cheese
$\frac{3}{4}$ cup margarine, softened
Salt to taste
1 cup grated Parmesan cheese

Combine the flour, cottage cheese, margarine and salt in a bowl; mix well.
Separate into 4 balls. Wrap each in plastic wrap. Chill for 1 hour to
overnight. Roll out each ball to an 8-inch circle on a floured surface.
Sprinkle each circle with $\frac{1}{4}$ cup of the Parmesan cheese. Cut the circles into
8 wedges; roll up into a crescent shape, turning the edges inward. Place
on a baking sheet. Bake at 375 degrees for 18 to 20 minutes
or until the edges are lightly browned.
Yield: 32 crescents.

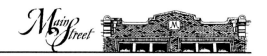

"Miss Sarah's" Corn Light Bread

*This recipe has passed through several generations of my
mother's family. Her name was Sarah, hence the name of the recipe.
I have found this particular recipe to be one of the best for corn
light bread, especially if fresh ground cornmeal is used.
My mother, whose family lived in the area that is now "Cool Springs,"
used to go to Readyville, Tennessee, to a mill there to have fresh
cornmeal for this wonderful bread.*

1 cup white cornmeal
1 cup all-purpose flour
$^1/_2$ cup sugar
$^1/_2$ teaspoon salt
2 teaspoons baking powder
1$^1/_4$ cups buttermilk
1 egg, beaten
3 tablespoons vegetable oil
1 tablespoon melted butter

Combine the cornmeal, flour, sugar, salt and baking powder in
a large bowl. Add the buttermilk, egg and oil, stirring after each
addition just until moistened. Pour into a 5x9-inch loaf pan sprayed
with cooking spray. Bake at 400 degrees for 30 to 40 minutes or until
lightly browned. Cool in the pan for 5 minutes; remove to a wire
rack to cool completely. Brush with butter.
Yield: 10 servings.

Lillie Mills, the producer
of White Lily Flour that
many southern cooks have
long favored for biscuit
making, was located in
Franklin for many years.
The mill burned to the
ground in 1958.

During the Battle of Franklin, a young boy named Hardin Figuers climbed a large tree near his home at Boxwood Hall on Main Street. From his perch Hardin had a bird's-eye view of the fierce battle until the fighting came so close to the house that he hid in the basement among the piles of potatoes.

Jalapeño Corn Bread

3 cups self-rising corn bread mix
2^1/$_2$ cups milk
^{1}/$_2$ cup vegetable oil
2 tablespoons sugar
^{1}/$_2$ cup chopped jalapeños, or to taste
1^1/$_2$ cups shredded sharp Cheddar cheese
4 ounces bacon, crisp-fried, crumbled
^{1}/$_4$ cup chopped pimentos
1 clove garlic, crushed
1 cup cream-style corn
1 large onion, grated
3 eggs, beaten

Combine the corn bread mix and milk in a large bowl. Stir in the oil, sugar, jalapeños, cheese, bacon, pimentos, garlic, corn, onion and eggs. Pour into 2 preheated greased cast-iron skillets. Bake at 450 degrees for 30 to 35 minutes or until lightly browned.
Yield: 16 servings.

Apricot Bread

This bread is delicious toasted, buttered, and served with coffee.

1¹/2 cups dried apricots
¹/2 cup butter, softened
1 cup sugar
2 eggs, beaten
³/4 cup orange juice
2 cups sifted all-purpose flour
1 tablespoon baking powder
¹/4 teaspoon baking soda
³/4 teaspoon salt
1 teaspoon grated orange peel
1 cup chopped walnuts

Soak the apricots in water to cover for 30 minutes. Drain and chop into bite-sized pieces; set aside. Cream the butter and sugar in a mixer bowl until light and fluffy. Add the eggs and orange juice alternately to the creamed mixture, mixing well after each addition. Add the flour, baking powder, baking soda, salt, orange peel and walnuts, stirring well. Grease a 5x9-inch loaf pan. Line the pan with foil and grease the foil. Pour in the batter. Bake at 350 degrees for 1¹/2 hours or until the bread tests done.
Yield: 12 servings.

After the fighting ended, Hardin's home was filled with wounded soldiers. The boy bandaged wounds and cared for the men by himself until his mother and sisters returned from their hiding place.

Franklin's early merchants operated their businesses, which they called "stands," by generously extending credit to their customers. Often the stands went bankrupt when the credit was not repaid. Early newspapers were full of ads asking the townspeople to come and pay their debts.

Mrs. Regen's Home-Baked Bread

We lived next door to Mrs. Regen. My two daughters played outside near her kitchen window. Often they would come inside and ask, "May we go to see Mrs. Regen?" "Why? I would ask. Answer, "She is cooking bread." The aroma is more powerful than any perfume you have experienced. My answer was always "Yes." I think Mrs. Regen would always raise her kitchen window to tempt them.

1 quart milk
1 cup sugar
1 cup shortening
2 envelopes dry yeast
1/2 cup lukewarm water
9 cups all-purpose flour
2 teaspoons baking powder
1 teaspoon baking soda
1 teaspoon salt
Butter or margarine, softened

Combine the milk, sugar and shortening in a saucepan. Bring to a boil, stirring until the sugar dissolves. Remove from heat and cool to lukewarm. Dissolve the yeast in lukewarm water. Combine the milk mixture and yeast in a large bowl. Sift the flour, baking powder, baking soda and salt together. Add to the milk mixture, stirring until smooth. Let rise 4 or 5 times, stirring down after each rising. Turn onto a floured surface. Knead for several minutes or until the dough is smooth and elastic. Shape into a long roll; cut into 4 portions. Place each portion in a greased loaf pan. Let rise, covered, until doubled in bulk. Bake at 350 degrees on the middle oven rack for 35 to 40 minutes or until the loaves are well browned and sound hollow when thumped on bottom. Remove from the oven and brush tops with butter. Cover the loaves still in pans with foil and a towel. Let stand until cooled. Of course if you prefer the bread hot, "Goodness gracious, it is good."
Yield: 4 loaves.

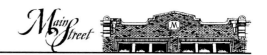

Cheese Pepper Bread

1 envelope dry yeast
$^1/_4$ cup hot water
$2^1/_3$ cups all-purpose flour
1 teaspoon salt
2 tablespoons sugar
$^1/_4$ teaspoon baking soda
1 cup sour cream
1 egg
1 cup shredded Cheddar cheese
$^1/_2$ teaspoon pepper

Dissolve the yeast in hot water in a large mixer bowl. Add $1^1/_3$ cups
of the flour, salt, sugar, baking soda, sour cream and egg. Beat at
low speed for 30 seconds, scraping the side of the bowl frequently. Beat at
high speed for 2 minutes. Add the remaining flour, cheese and pepper,
mixing well. Grease two 1-pound coffee cans. Pour an equal amount of the
batter into the cans. Let rise, covered, in a warm place for 50 minutes
or until doubled in bulk. Bake at 350 degrees for 40 minutes or until the
loaves are golden brown, will slip easily from the cans and sound
hollow when thumped on the bottom. Remove from the cans
immediately and place on wire racks to cool.
Yield: 2 loaves.

The residents of Franklin
in the 1830s had a taste
for reading. The Franklin
Literary Club met regularly
at Masonic Hall during
those years.

Main Street is a designated historic district and is on the National Register of Historic Places. In 1985 Franklin was named a National Trust Main Street.

Onion and Cheese Bread

$^1\!/_2$ cup chopped onion
1 tablespoon vegetable oil
1 egg, slightly beaten
$^1\!/_2$ cup milk
$1^1\!/_4$ cups Bisquick
1 cup shredded sharp Cheddar cheese
1 tablespoon poppy seeds
2 tablespoons melted margarine

Sauté the onion in oil in a small skillet until golden brown. Beat the egg and milk in a large bowl. Stir in the baking mix, sautéed onion and $^1\!/_2$ cup of the cheese. Spread the dough into a greased 8-inch round baking pan. Sprinkle with the remaining cheese and poppy seeds. Pour melted margarine over the top. Bake at 400 degrees for 20 to 25 minutes or until the bread tests done. Serve hot.
Yield: 6 servings.

Magnificent Cheese Muffins

$1^1\!/_2$ cups all-purpose flour
2 tablespoons baking powder
$^1\!/_2$ teaspoon salt
2 tablespoons sugar
1 cup shredded Cheddar cheese
1 egg, beaten
1 cup milk
$^1\!/_2$ cup melted margarine

Combine the flour, baking powder, salt and sugar in a large bowl. Stir in the cheese; make a well in the center. Add the egg, milk and margarine, stirring well. Pour into greased muffin cups, filling $^2\!/_3$ full. Bake at 400 degrees for 20 to 25 minutes or until golden brown. Cool on a wire rack.
Yield: 12 servings.

Sour Cream Corn Muffins

1 cup self-rising yellow cornmeal mix
$^1/_2$ teaspoon salt
$^1/_4$ cup vegetable oil
1 (8-ounce) can cream-style corn
1 cup sour cream
2 eggs, slightly beaten

Combine the cornmeal, salt, oil, corn, sour cream and eggs in a
large bowl; mix well. Pour into greased muffin cups, filling $^2/_3$ full. Bake
at 400 degrees for 25 minutes. Cool on a wire rack.
Yield: 12 servings.

Morning Glory Muffins

2 cups all-purpose flour
$1^1/_4$ cups sugar
2 teaspoons (scant) baking soda
2 teaspoons cinnamon
$^1/_2$ teaspoon salt
2 cups grated carrots
$^1/_2$ cup raisins
$^1/_2$ cup each chopped pecans and shredded coconut
1 apple, peeled, cored, grated
3 eggs
1 cup vegetable oil
2 teaspoons vanilla extract

Combine the flour, sugar, baking soda, cinnamon and salt in a large bowl.
Stir in the carrots, raisins, pecans, coconut and apple. Beat the eggs
with oil and vanilla in a bowl. Add to the flour mixture, stirring just until
moistened. Pour into greased muffin cups. Bake at 350 degrees
for 20 minutes. Cool on a wire rack.
Yield: 14 muffins.

*L*ike many early
physicians, Dr. Daniel
McPhail sold medications
from his Main Street office.
One of the medicines he
advertised was a "medicated
sherry" which was used as a
"restorative" for females.

Never-Fail Rolls

This recipe was given to me by Mrs. Ed Ladd, a Franklin resident. I have used it for years and always make them for family dinners.

1 envelope dry yeast
1/2 cup lukewarm water
1 cup mashed potatoes
1/2 cup sugar
2 eggs
1 teaspoon salt
2/3 cup vegetable oil
1 cup scalded milk
5 to 6 cups all-purpose flour
Melted butter

Dissolve the yeast in lukewarm water; set aside. Combine the mashed potatoes and sugar in a large mixer bowl, beating at medium speed until well blended. Beat in eggs 1 at a time. Add the salt, oil, milk and yeast 1 at a time, beating well after each addition. Add 4 cups flour and mix well. Add enough of the remaining 2 cups flour gradually to make a dough that is firm but not stiff. Shape dough into a ball. Oil a large bowl. Place dough in prepared bowl, turning to coat surface. Refrigerate, loosely covered, for several hours to overnight. Knead lightly on a floured surface. Roll lightly to 1/2-inch thickness. Cut with a small biscuit cutter. Arrange on lightly greased baking sheets. Let rise, loosely covered, in a warm place for 2 hours or until doubled in bulk. Brush with melted butter. Bake at 400 degrees for 8 to 10 minutes or until golden brown.
Yield: 3 to 4 dozen rolls.

Vegetables

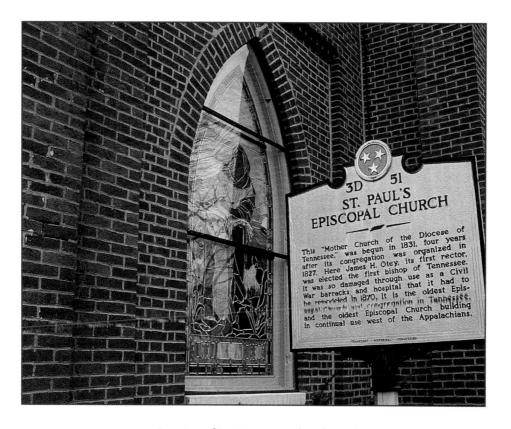

St. Paul's Episcopal Church

Vegetables

Dolly Parton's Cowboy Beans...133
Hot Baked Beans...133
Cabbage Casserole...134
Carrot Casserole...134
Baby Carrots with Tarragon Glaze...135
Green-Moore House Corn Pudding...135
Couscous with Vegetables...136
Green Bean Bundles...136
Green Beans with Balsamic Pesto...137
Old-Fashioned Mushrooms...137
Grilled Red Onions...138
Green Pea Tarts...138
*Mashed Potatoes and Parsnips
with Parsley...139*
Roasted Orange Potatoes...139
Roasted Potato Salad...140

St. Paul's Episcopal Church

The beautiful Mother Church of the Episcopal Diocese of Tennessee was constructed in 1834. After the Battle of Franklin the church was heavily damaged by the Union Army. The pews and pulpit were burned and holes were chopped in both the ceiling and pillars. The altar silver had been buried in the yard and was thus spared. After the war the building was remodeled and repaired with donations from churches in the North. The ceiling was lowered at that time and the slave galleries were removed.

Early in the twentieth century the church received its beautiful Tiffany windows. Charles Tiffany, the creator of the windows, died without revealing the formula for creating his beautiful stained glass. Thus, St. Paul's windows are a priceless and irreplaceable treasure.

During World War I the bells from the tower were melted to make cannons for the war effort. St. Paul's has been in continuous use for over 150 years, and is an island of serenity in today's hectic world.

St. Paul's Church is located at 510 West Main Street.

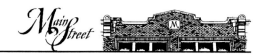

Dolly Parton's Cowboy Beans

1 pound ground beef
2 medium onions, finely chopped
1 small green bell pepper, finely chopped
2 (16-ounce) cans pork and beans, or 4 cups fresh October beans
2 cups catsup
1 teaspoon vinegar
$1/4$ cup packed brown sugar
2 teaspoons prepared mustard
1 teaspoon each salt and pepper

Cook the first 3 ingredients in a 10-inch skillet until brown and crumbly; drain. Stir in the remaining ingredients. Pour into a baking dish. Bake at 350 degrees for 20 minutes.
Yield: 8 to 10 servings.

Hot Baked Beans

$3^1/2$ cups dried Great Northern white beans, rinsed, sorted
1 (4-ounce) smoked ham hock
$3^1/2$ teaspoons salt
1 large onion, finely chopped
$1^1/4$ cups prepared tomato-based barbecue sauce
1 (12-ounce) jar tomato-based hot salsa
$1/3$ cup packed brown sugar
$1/4$ cup each Dijon mustard and light unsulphured molasses

Combine beans with water to cover in a Dutch oven. Bring to a boil. Remove from heat. Let stand for 1 hour; drain. Add water to cover and ham hock. Simmer for 20 minutes. Add 2 teaspoons salt. Simmer for 20 minutes or until tender. Drain, reserving $1^1/2$ cups cooking liquid.
Combine the beans, ham hock, cooking liquid and remaining ingredients in the Dutch oven. Bake, covered, at 350 degrees for 1 hour. Bake, uncovered, for 40 minutes, stirring occasionally.
Yield: 8 to 10 servings.

*H*arlinsdale Stables, located on Franklin Road just north of town, was once home of *Midnight Sun*, 1945 and 1946 World's Grand Champion Walking Horse.

Cabbage Casserole

1 medium head cabbage, chopped
6 tablespoons each butter and all-purpose flour
3 cups milk
1 onion, chopped
Salt and pepper to taste
12 ounces Cheddar cheese, grated
1¹/₂ cups herb-seasoned stuffing mix
Margarine

Place the cabbage in a saucepan with enough water to cover. Cook for
10 minutes; drain and set aside. Melt the butter in a small saucepan; remove
from heat. Stir in the flour. Add the milk gradually; add the onion, salt
and pepper. Cook over low heat until the mixture thickens, stirring constantly. Layer the cabbage, cheese and sauce in a 9x13-inch buttered baking
dish. Top with the herb stuffing mix; dot with margarine. Bake at 350
degrees for 30 to 45 minutes or until heated through.
Yield: 6 to 8 servings.

Carrot Casserole

2 pounds carrots, sliced
Salt to taste
8 ounces Velveeta cheese
8 tablespoons butter or margarine
16 Ritz crackers, crumbled

Place the carrots in a saucepan with enough salted water to cover. Cook for
15 to 20 minutes or until tender; drain. Spoon into a greased 9x13-inch
baking dish. Melt cheese and 6 tablespoons of the butter in a saucepan over
low heat; pour over the carrots. Melt the remaining 2 tablespoons butter.
Toss the crackers in the butter to coat lightly. Sprinkle over the carrots. Bake
at 350 degrees for 15 to 20 minutes or until the mixture is bubbly.
Yield: 6 servings.

Baby Carrots with Tarragon Glaze

4 bunches baby carrots (with stems)
$1/4$ cup water
3 tablespoons minced fresh tarragon
2 tablespoons butter
1 tablespoon white wine vinegar
1 tablespoon honey
Salt and pepper to taste

Trim the carrots, leaving a 3-inch stem. Place in a saucepan with
the water, $1^{1}/_{2}$ tablespoons of the tarragon, the butter, vinegar and honey.
Bring to a boil; reduce heat to medium. Simmer, covered, for
12 minutes or until the carrots are tender-crisp and slightly glazed. Cook,
uncovered, for 6 minutes longer. Season with salt, pepper and
the remaining $1^{1}/_{2}$ tablespoons tarragon.
Yield: 6 servings.

Green-Moore House Corn Pudding

2 cups canned cream-style corn
3 tablespoons all-purpose flour
1 tablespoon melted butter
1 tablespoon sugar
1 teaspoon salt
3 eggs, well beaten
2 cups milk

Combine the corn, flour, butter, sugar and salt in a bowl and
mix well. Add the eggs and stir until well mixed. Stir in the milk gradually.
Pour into a greased $1^{1}/_{2}$-quart casserole. Bake at 350 degrees for
15 to 20 minutes. Stir the casserole. Bake for 25 to 30 minutes longer
or just until the center of the casserole is set.
Yield: 6 servings.

Franklin was hit exceptionally hard by the "flood of the century" in 1975. Water rose up to five feet deep on Hillsboro Road and Lewisburg Pike was impassable.

Couscous with Vegetables

1 cup each chopped broccoli, carrots, new potatoes and yellow squash
3/4 cup olive oil
1 (6-ounce) package couscous
1/2 cup fresh lemon juice
2 cloves of garlic, minced
1 teaspoon Dijon mustard
1 teaspoon each coriander and salt
Pepper to taste

Sauté the broccoli, carrots, potatoes and squash in olive oil in a large skillet until tender. Prepare the couscous using package directions. Mix the lemon juice, garlic, mustard, coriander, salt and pepper in a small bowl. Combine with the vegetables and couscous in a medium bowl, mixing well. Serve warm.
Yield: 6 servings.

Green Bean Bundles

This is a favorite dish in our Franklin neighborhood and is always on the menu for special occasions, such as progressive dinners, farewell dinners, and birthdays.

1 (16-ounce) can whole green beans, drained
4 slices bacon, cut into halves
1 (4-ounce) jar sliced mushrooms, drained
Salt, pepper, garlic powder and Worcestershire sauce to taste

Arrange 6 green beans on each half slice of the bacon. Wrap up and secure with a wooden pick. Place the bundles in a medium baking dish; add the mushrooms. Sprinkle with salt, pepper, garlic powder and Worcestershire sauce. Bake at 375 degrees for 30 minutes or until the bacon is crisp. Remove wooden picks before serving.
Yield: 4 servings.

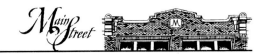

Green Beans with Balsamic Pesto

This is a wonderful side dish with grilled meat or fish.

1¹/₂ pounds fresh green beans, trimmed
²/₃ recipe pesto sauce (page 114), at room temperature
4 to 5 tablespoons balsamic vinegar
¹/₂ teaspoon brown sugar
Salt and pepper to taste

Steam the green beans in a vegetable steamer for 6 minutes or until tender-crisp. Place in a serving bowl. Spoon the pesto sauce over the beans. Mix the vinegar and brown sugar in a small bowl. Pour over the beans. Toss gently to coat. Season with salt and pepper. Serve warm or hot.
Yield: 6 servings.

Old-Fashioned Mushrooms

¹/₄ cup butter
10 ounces large mushrooms, cut into quarters
2 cloves of garlic, minced
1 tablespoon all-purpose flour
1 cup milk
2 tablespoons whipping cream
Salt and pepper to taste
1¹/₂ tablespoons chopped fresh parsley

Melt the butter in a large heavy skillet over medium-high heat. Add the mushrooms. Sauté for 15 minutes or until golden brown. Add the garlic. Sauté for 1 minute. Sprinkle with 1 tablespoon of the flour, stirring to coat. Add the milk and cream. Bring to a boil, stirring constantly; reduce heat. Simmer for 8 minutes or until the mixture is thickened, stirring often. Season with the salt and pepper; sprinkle with the parsley.
Yield: 2 servings.

Grilled Red Onions

4 medium red onions
$2^{1}/_{4}$ tablespoons Worcestershire sauce
2 tablespoon balsamic or red wine vinegar
2 tablespoons soy sauce
2 tablespoons olive oil
$^{3}/_{4}$ teaspoon pepper

Cut a $^{1}/_{4}$-inch slice off the top and bottom of each onion and discard.
Cut the onions into halves crosswise. Arrange in a single layer in a shallow
dish. Whisk the Worcestershire sauce, vinegar, soy sauce and olive oil in a
small bowl. Pour over the onions. Marinate for 1 hour; drain. Grill the
onions for 4 minutes on each side. Season with pepper.
Yield: 4 servings.

Green Pea Tarts

8 miniature tart shells
$^{1}/_{4}$ cup margarine
2 tablespoons all-purpose flour
1 (5-ounce) can evaporated milk
$^{1}/_{4}$ cup milk
1 (16-ounce) can tiny baby peas, drained
1 (4-ounce) can sliced mushrooms, drained
4 ounces Cheddar cheese, shredded

Bake the shells using package directions; set aside. Melt the
margarine in a medium saucepan. Stir in the flour, evaporated milk and
milk slowly. Cook over medium heat until thickened, stirring
constantly. Add the peas, mushrooms, salt and pepper, stirring to coat.
Spoon into the prepared shells. Sprinkle with the cheese. Bake at
350 degrees for 15 to 20 minutes or until bubbly.
Yield: 8 servings.

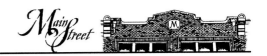

Mashed Potatoes and Parsnips with Parsley

1¹/₂ pounds gold potatoes, peeled, cut into 2-inch pieces
1 pound parsnips, peeled, cut into 1¹/₂-inch pieces
3 ounces parsley root, trimmed, peeled, cut into 1-inch pieces
1 clove of garlic, cut into halves
1 (14-ounce) can low-salt chicken broth
3 cups (about) water
¹/₄ cup whipping cream
2 tablespoons each butter and minced parsley
Salt and pepper to taste

Combine the first 4 ingredients in a large heavy saucepan. Add broth and
enough water to cover. Cook, covered, over high heat for 30 minutes or
until tender; drain, reserving liquid. Add the cream and butter. Cook over
low heat, beating until the mixture is light and fluffy, adding enough
reserved liquid gradually to make of desired consistency. Stir in parsley, salt
and pepper. Spoon into a serving bowl. Garnish with additional parsley.
Yield: 6 servings.

Roasted Orange Potatoes

3 medium red potatoes, scrubbed
1 teaspoon minced orange peel
2 teaspoons extra-virgin olive oil
¹/₂ teaspoon dried rubbed sage
¹/₄ teaspoon pepper
Salt to taste

Cut each potato into 8 wedges. Toss in a mixture of the remaining
ingredients until coated. Arrange the potato wedges on a baking sheet,
leaving a space between. Bake at 425 degrees for 40 minutes or
until crisp and brown, turning once.
Yield: 4 servings.

During the big blizzard of 1951, the damage to telephone lines was so massive that assistance had to be brought in from Kentucky.

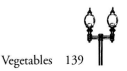

Roasted Potato Salad

4 ounces bacon, coarsely chopped
1 cup plus 1 tablespoon olive oil
$2/3$ cup chopped shallots
$1^1/_2$ teaspoons dried thyme
$^1/_4$ cup white wine vinegar
$^1/_8$ teaspoon saffron
$^1/_4$ cup chopped fresh tarragon
Salt and pepper to taste
8 small red potatoes
8 ounces shiitake mushrooms
8 ounces oyster mushrooms
12 ounces green beans, trimmed
16 cups assorted baby salad greens
2 large heads Belgian endive, sliced

Cook the bacon in a heavy skillet until crispy. Drain on a paper
towel and set aside. Add 1 tablespoon of the olive oil, shallots and thyme to
the pan drippings. Sauté for 2 minutes. Stir in the vinegar and saffron.
Remove from heat. Whisk in the remaining olive oil and tarragon. Season
with salt and pepper. Cut each of the potatoes into 6 wedges; place in
a medium bowl. Combine shiitake and oyster mushrooms in another
medium bowl. Pour $^1/_4$ of the dressing over potatoes and $^1/_4$ over
mushrooms, tossing to coat. Season with salt and pepper. Arrange the
potatoes and mushrooms on two separate baking sheets. Let stand for 30
minutes at room temperature. Roast the potatoes at 400 degrees
for 40 minutes or until browned and crispy, turning once. Roast the
mushrooms for 15 minutes or until browned and crispy, turning once.
Cook the green beans in boiling salted water in a large saucepan for
4 minutes or until tender-crisp; drain. Rinse under cold water and drain
again. Combine with the potatoes, mushrooms, salad greens and
endive in a large bowl. Toss with the remaining dressing;
sprinkle with the reserved bacon.
Yield: 8 to 10 servings.

Desserts

Carnton Plantation

Desserts

Carnton Plantation

Carnton was completed in 1826. It is a Greek Revival style house with some Georgian and Federal influences. It was built by Randal McGavock. He served as mayor of Nashville from 1824 to 1825.

Carnton Plantation was known for its beautiful gardens. Randal's wife Sarah was close friends with Rachel Jackson and it is believed that Rachel shared cuttings from the gardens at The Hermitage with Sarah.

Upon inheriting the home in 1843, John McGavock made renovations to the home, including building the back veranda for his wife Caroline, reminiscent of the homes in her native Louisiana.

Carnton's place in history is secured by its significance following the Battle of Franklin. John and Caroline McGavock opened their home to hundreds of wounded soldiers. Caroline's mercy knew no bounds, as evidenced by this letter from a Confederate soldier to his wife, dated January 14, 1865.

"Every room was filled, every bed had two bleeding fellows, every spare space, niche and corner, under the stairs, in the hall, everywhere but one room for her family. And when the noble old house could hold no more, the yard was appropriated until the wounded and dead filled that, and all were not provided for. Our doctors were deficient in bandages, and she began by giving her old linen, then her towels and napkins, then her sheets and tablecloths, and then her husband's shirts and her own undergarments."

Carnton Plantation is now maintained by the Carnton Association. The house has been restored to its former beauty and is open to the public. It is located at 1345 Carnton Lane.

Carrot Cake

2 cups all-purpose flour
2 teaspoons baking soda
1 teaspoon salt
1 teaspoon cinnamon
2 cups sugar
4 eggs, slightly beaten
1^1/$_2$ cups vegetable oil
1 (8-ounce) can crushed pineapple, drained
^{3}/$_4$ cup walnut pieces
3 (4-ounce) jars baby food carrots
1 (1-pound) package confectioners' sugar
^{1}/$_2$ cup butter, softened
1 teaspoon vanilla extract
8 ounces cream cheese, softened
Milk

Mix the flour, baking soda, salt, cinnamon and sugar in a bowl.
Add the eggs, oil, pineapple, walnuts and carrots and mix well. Pour into a
greased 9x13-inch cake pan. Bake at 350 degrees for 55 minutes.
Sift the confectioners' sugar into a mixer bowl. Add the butter, vanilla and
cream cheese and beat well. Beat in enough milk to make of
spreading consistency. Spread over the warm cake.
Yield: 12 servings.

Franklin's *Review Appeal*
is the oldest continuously run
newspaper in Tennessee.
Originally it was called the
Western Weekly Review.

Apricot Nectar Cake

4 eggs
1 cup apricot nectar
1 cup vegetable oil
$^1/_2$ cup sugar
1 (2-layer) package lemon cake mix
1 cup confectioners' sugar
2 teaspoons lemon juice

Combine the eggs, apricot nectar, oil, sugar and cake mix in a bowl
and mix well. Pour into a greased bundt pan. Bake at 350 degrees for 45 to
55 minutes or until the cake tests done. Cool in the pan for several
minutes. Invert onto a serving plate. Mix the confectioners' sugar and
lemon juice in a bowl until very smooth. Pour over the warm cake.
Yield: 12 to 16 servings.

Best Fudge Cake Ever

This recipe was made famous by Geneva Bryan of Nashville.

1 cup margarine, softened
2 cups sugar
4 eggs
1 cup (scant) all-purpose flour
$^1/_2$ cup baking cocoa
$^1/_4$ teaspoon salt
1 teaspoon vanilla extract
1 cup chopped pecans or walnuts

Cream the margarine and sugar in a mixer bowl until light and fluffy.
Beat in the eggs 1 at a time. Add the flour, cocoa, salt and vanilla and beat
well. Stir in the pecans. Pour into a greased 8x14-inch cake pan. Bake
at 300 degrees for 45 minutes. Do not preheat the oven.
Yield: 36 servings.

Mimmama's Fresh Coconut Cake

1 large fresh coconut
3 cups sifted cake flour
1 tablespoon baking powder
$3/4$ cup shortening
2 teaspoons vanilla extract
$3/4$ teaspoon salt
2 cups sugar
$1^1/3$ cups milk
6 egg whites, stiffly beaten
Fluffy Frosting (see below)

Drain the coconut, reserving 1 to 2 tablespoons coconut milk. Strain the coconut milk. Peel and finely grate the coconut meat. Sift the cake flour and baking powder together. Beat the next 3 ingredients in a bowl. Add the sugar gradually, beating until fluffy. Beat in the flour mixture and milk alternately. Fold in the egg whites. Pour into 3 greased and floured 8-inch round cake pans. Bake at 350 degrees for 25 minutes or until the layers test done.

Cool in the pans for several minutes. Remove to a wire rack to cool completely. Pierce the layers with a fork 10 to 12 times. Drizzle with the coconut milk. Spread with frosting, sprinkling each layer with coconut.
Yield: 12 to 16 servings.

Fluffy Frosting

2 cups sugar
$2/3$ cup water
$1/2$ teaspoon cream of tartar
4 egg whites
1 teaspoon each vanilla and almond extract

Cook the the first 3 ingredients in a heavy saucepan over low heat until the syrup spins a 6- to 8-inch thread; do not stir. Beat the egg whites in a mixer bowl until soft peaks form. Add the syrup gradually, beating constantly. Beat in flavorings.

Mimmama was Blanche Sevier Bradford, a direct descendant of John Sevier, the first governor of Tennessee and a Revolutionary War hero. This recipe has been handed down in her line of the Sevier family for generations. An interesting note on the original recipe emphasizes that the flour must be sifted three times before measuring. Modern cake flour needs only one sifting. This cake is a must at Christmas garnished with fresh holly and berries.

The Williamson County Courthouse was erected in 1858 and is one of only a few Tennessee courthouses that were built before the Civil War. It is a good example of southern antebellum architecture.

GG's Gingerbread

3 eggs
1 cup each sugar and molasses
1 teaspoon each ground cloves, ginger and cinnamon
1 cup vegetable oil
2 teaspoons baking soda
2 tablespoons plus 1 cup boiling water
2 cups all-purpose flour, sifted

Beat the first 7 ingredients in a large bowl. Add baking soda dissolved in 2 tablespoons water. Beat in the flour. Add 1 cup water, beating lightly and quickly; batter will be thin. Pour into a greased 9x13-inch cake pan. Bake at 300 degrees for 1 hour. Cut into squares. Serve hot with whipped topping.
Yield: 12 servings.

Jam Cake

4 cups sifted all-purpose flour
2¹/₂ teaspoons baking powder
1¹/₂ teaspoons each cinnamon and allspice
1¹/₂ cups butter, softened
2 cups sugar
6 eggs, beaten
1 cup buttermilk
2 cups blackberry jam
1 (8-ounce) can crushed pineapple (undrained)
1 cup each raisins and chopped pecans

Sift the flour, baking powder and spices together. Cream the butter and sugar in a mixer bowl until fluffy. Beat in the eggs 1 at a time. Beat in the flour mixture and buttermilk alternately. Fold in the remaining ingredients. Pour into 3 greased and paper-lined 9-inch round cake pans. Bake at 350 degrees for 25 minutes or until the layers test done. Cool on wire rack. Store with a sliced apple for several days before frosting with a caramel icing.
Yield: 12 to 16 servings.

Million Dollar Pound Cake

3 cups sugar
2 cups butter, softened
6 eggs, at room temperature
4 cups all-purpose flour
3/4 cup milk
1 teaspoon each almond and vanilla extract, or 2 teaspoons lemon extract

Cream the sugar and butter in a bowl until light and fluffy. Beat in the eggs 1 at a time. Beat in the flour and milk alternately. Stir in the extracts. Pour into a greased and floured tube pan. Bake at 300 degrees for 1 hour and 40 minutes or until a toothpick inserted in center comes out clean.
Yield: 16 servings.

Pumpkin Roll

3 eggs, beaten
1 cup sugar
1 teaspoon each salt and baking soda
1/2 teaspoon cinnamon
3/4 cup all-purpose flour
2/3 cup pumpkin
Confectioners' sugar
8 ounces cream cheese, softened
1 teaspoon vanilla extract
2 tablespoons butter, softened
1 cup confectioners' sugar

Mix the first 7 ingredients in a bowl. Pour into a greased and waxed-paper-lined jelly roll pan. Bake at 350 degrees for 15 minutes or until brown. Invert onto a towel sprinkled with confectioners' sugar; remove paper. Roll up the cake with the towel lengthwise. Cool for several minutes; unroll and remove the towel. Spread with a mixture of remaining ingredients and reroll. Wrap in plastic wrap and then in foil. Chill until serving time.
Yield: 15 servings.

Before the passage of the penitentiary law in 1829, criminals were punished in front of the old courthouse which stood in the center of the square. Commonly used punishments included whipping, branding, or hanging. Franklin legend recounts the hanging of criminals from the iron railing on the courthouse porch.

Desserts 147

Robert Rainey, a merchant during the early 1800s, had his coffin built and used it to hold apples and potatoes in his store. When Mr. Rainey died, the vegetables and fruits were removed and the coffin was put to its intended use.

Fresh Pear Cake

3 cups all-purpose flour
1 teaspoon each baking soda and salt
2 cups sugar
3 eggs, beaten
1^1/$_2$ cups vegetable oil
1 teaspoon vanilla extract
2 teaspoons ground cinnamon
3 cups thinly sliced pears
1 cup packed brown sugar
^{1}/$_2$ cup butter or margarine
^{1}/$_4$ cup milk

Mix the flour, baking soda and salt together. Combine the sugar, eggs and oil in a bowl and mix well. Add the flour mixture 1 cup at a time, mixing well after each addition. Stir in the vanilla, cinnamon and pears. Spoon into a greased 10-inch bundt pan. Bake at 350 degrees for 1^1/$_4$ hours or until the cake tests done. Bring the remaining ingredients to a boil in a saucepan. Boil for 3 minutes. Pour over the hot cake in the pan.
Yield: 16 servings.

Praline Sauce

3 tablespoons butter or margarine
1 cup packed brown sugar
^{1}/$_2$ cup half-and-half
1 cup chopped pecans
1 teaspoon vanilla extract

Melt the butter in a heavy saucepan over low heat. Add the brown sugar. Cook for 5 to 8 minutes, stirring constantly. Remove from the heat. Stir in the half-and-half gradually. Cook for 1 minute, stirring constantly. Remove from the heat; add pecans and vanilla. Serve over pound cake or ice cream.
Yield: 1^1/$_2$ cups.

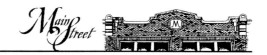

Marshmallow Brownies

1/2 cup plus 1 tablespoon butter
4 tablespoons baking cocoa
2 eggs, beaten
1 cup each sugar and chopped pecans
2/3 cup all-purpose flour
1 package miniature marshmallows
1/2 to 1 (1-pound) package confectioners' sugar
2 to 3 tablespoons light cream or milk

Melt 1/2 cup of the butter and 2 tablespoons of the baking cocoa in a saucepan, stirring constantly. Add to the eggs. Add sugar and mix well. Stir in the pecans and flour. Pour into a greased 6x9-inch glass baking dish. Bake at 350 degrees for 25 minutes or until the brownies test done. Sprinkle with the marshmallows, pressing together. Melt remaining butter and baking cocoa in a saucepan. Add confectioners' sugar and cream and beat until of spreading consistency. Spread over marshmallows.
Yield: 12 servings.

Date Nut Balls

1/2 cup each sugar and packed brown sugar
1/2 cup margarine
1/8 teaspoon salt
1 (8-ounce) package chopped dates
1 teaspoon vanilla extract
2 cups crisp rice cereal
1 cup each coconut and chopped pecans or walnuts
Confectioners' sugar

Boil the first 5 ingredients in a saucepan for 5 minutes, stirring constantly. Remove from the heat and beat in vanilla. Fold in the cereal, coconut and pecans. Shape into balls. Roll in confectioners' sugar. Dry on waxed paper.
Yield: 5 dozen.

During the latter half of the 19th century, an ex-slave named Harry Marsh made his living operating a taxi service between the old train depot and the square. The children of the town would wait for "Uncle Harry" on the side of Third Avenue. Often they were rewarded with a chance to ride in Uncle Harry's hack and hold the reins.

Fudgy Oatmeal Bars

2 cups packed brown sugar
1 cup margarine, softened
2 eggs
1 teaspoon vanilla extract
2$^1/_2$ cups all-purpose flour
1 teaspoon baking soda
$^1/_2$ teaspoon salt
3 cups quick-cooking oats
2 cups semisweet chocolate chips (12 ounces)
1 (14-ounce) can sweetened condensed milk
2 tablespoons margarine
1 teaspoon vanilla extract
$^1/_2$ teaspoon salt
1 cup chopped pecans or walnuts

Combine the brown sugar, 1 cup margarine, eggs and 1 teaspoon vanilla in a large bowl and mix well. Stir in the flour, baking soda and $^1/_2$ teaspoon salt. Stir in the oats. Reserve $^1/_3$ of the oat mixture. Press the remaining oat mixture into a 10x15-inch jelly roll pan. Combine the chocolate chips, condensed milk and 2 tablespoons margarine in a saucepan. Cook over low heat until the chocolate is melted, stirring constantly. Remove from the heat. Stir in 1 teaspoon vanilla, $^1/_2$ teaspoon salt and the pecans. Spread over the oat mixture in the pan. Drop the reserved oat mixture by rounded teaspoonfuls onto the chocolate mixture. Bake at 350 degrees for 25 to 30 minutes or until golden brown. Cut into bars while warm.

Yield: 5 dozen.

Praline Bars

1/3 (16-ounce) package honey-flavored graham crackers
1 cup butter (no substitutions)
1/2 cup sugar
3/4 cup pecan pieces

Break the graham crackers into 3 sections. Line a 10x15-inch jelly roll pan with the crackers. Bring the butter and sugar to a boil in a saucepan. Boil for 3 minutes, stirring constantly. Pour evenly over the crackers. Sprinkle with the pecans. Bake at 350 degrees for 12 minutes. Cool for several minutes. Remove from the pan with a spatula and cool on waxed paper or foil. May sprinkle with 1 package of chocolate chips after baking.
Yield: 40 servings.

Santa's Whiskers

1 cup butter, softened (no substitutions)
1 cup sugar
2 tablespoons milk
1 teaspoon vanilla extract
2 1/2 cups self-rising flour
3/4 cup chopped red cherries
3/4 cup chopped green cherries
1/2 cup chopped pecans
3/4 cup coconut

Cream the butter and sugar in a mixer bowl until light and fluffy. Add the milk and vanilla and mix well. Stir in the flour, cherries, pecans and coconut. Shape into 2 rolls. Chill for several hours. Cut the rolls into 1/4-inch-thick slices. Place on a nonstick cookie sheet.
Bake at 375 degrees for 12 minutes.
Yield: 5 dozen.

*T*his recipe is an encore presentation from *Flaunting Our Finest*, Junior of Auxiliary of Franklin's first cookbook.

In the days when many Franklin residents had cooks, they ruled their kitchens with an iron hand. Children were often forbidden to enter the kitchen area. One favorite cook in town, known as Aunt Jane, compensated for this by allowing children to line up at the kitchen window where she gave them freshly baked tea cakes cut into the shapes of men and women.

Great-Great-Grandmother's Tea Cakes

1 cup butter, softened
$2^1/2$ cups sugar
2 eggs, beaten
1 tablespoon milk (optional)
1 teaspoon vanilla extract
1 teaspoon baking soda
1 teaspoon cinnamon (optional)
$4^1/4$ cups all-purpose flour

Cream the butter and sugar in a mixer bowl until light and fluffy. Add the eggs, milk, vanilla, baking soda and cinnamon and mix well. Add enough of the flour to make a soft dough, mixing well after each addition. Roll $1/8$ inch thick on a floured surface. Cut with a 2- to 3-inch cookie cutter. Place on a nonstick cookie sheet. Bake at 400 degrees for 10 minutes or until lightly browned.
Yield: 5 to 6 dozen.

Whiskey Sauce

$2/3$ cup packed brown sugar
2 tablespoons light corn syrup
$1/4$ cup water
$1/4$ cup butter
1 blade of mace
$1/2$ cup whiskey

Combine the brown sugar, corn syrup, water, butter and mace in a double boiler. Cook over boiling water until thickened, stirring frequently. Remove from the heat and stir in the whiskey. Serve over sweet potatoes or date nut bars.
Yield: 10 to 20 servings.

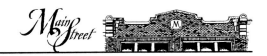

Coconut Meringue Pies

6 eggs, separated
3/4 cup milk
1 1/2 cups sugar
1 1/2 teaspoons all-purpose flour
3/4 cup melted butter
1 cup flaked coconut
1 teaspoon vanilla extract
2 unbaked (8-inch) pie shells
1/2 cup sugar

Mix the egg yolks and milk in a medium bowl. Add 1 1/2 cups sugar,
flour and butter and mix by hand until smooth. Stir in the coconut and
vanilla. Pour into the pie shells. Bake at 350 degrees for 30 to 35 minutes
or until lightly browned and set. Beat the egg whites in a mixer bowl until
stiff peaks form. Add 1/2 cup sugar, beating constantly. Spread over the pies,
sealing to the edge. Bake at 400 degrees until lightly browned.
Yield: 12 to 16 servings.

Frozen Key Lime Pie

1/2 cup lime juice
Grated zest of 1 lime
1 (14-ounce) can sweetened condensed milk
8 ounces whipped topping
2 tablespoons Grand Marnier
1 chocolate crumb pie shell

Mix the lime juice, zest and condensed milk in a bowl. Fold in the whipped
topping. Stir in the liqueur. Spoon into the pie shell. Freeze for 8 to 10
hours. Let stand for several minutes before serving.
Yield: 6 to 8 servings.

During the 1950s and
1960s the largest concrete
swimming pool in the South
was located in Franklin.
Willow Plunge featured two
spring-fed pools, a picnic
pavilion and a grassy bank
for sunbathing. It was a
favorite summer hangout for
residents of Franklin and the
surrounding area.

Lemon Chess Pie

2 cups sugar
1 tablespoon all-purpose flour
1 tablespoon cornmeal
4 eggs, beaten
$1/4$ cup melted butter
$1/4$ cup milk
$1/4$ cup fresh lemon juice
Grated peel of 1 lemon
1 unbaked (9-inch) pie shell

Mix the sugar, flour and cornmeal in a large bowl. Add the eggs,
butter, milk, lemon juice and lemon peel and mix well. Pour into the
pie shell. Bake at 450 degrees for 10 minutes. Reduce the oven
temperature to 350 degrees. Bake for 30 minutes longer. Serve at room
temperature or slightly chilled.
Yield: 6 to 8 servings.

Pie Crusts

3 cups sifted all-purpose flour
1 teaspoon salt
1 cup butter-flavored shortening
1 egg yolk, beaten
9 tablespoons milk

Combine the flour and salt in a bowl. Cut in the shortening with
a pastry blender until resembles coarse crumbs. Add the egg yolk and milk
and mix until a soft dough forms. Shape into a ball. Chill for 30 minutes or
longer. Divide the ball into 2 portions. Roll each into a circle on a
floured surface. Fit each circle into a 9-inch pie plate, trimming
and fluting the edge. Bake at 375 degrees for 20 to 25 minutes
or until browned. Freezes well.
Yield: 2 (9-inch) pie crusts.

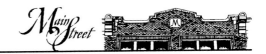

Fudge Pie

This pie is very rich and may be cut into smaller servings.

1 cup sugar
$^1/_3$ cup all-purpose flour
$^1/_8$ teaspoon salt
$^1/_2$ cup melted butter or margarine
2 egg yolks
1 teaspoon vanilla extract
2 ounces semisweet chocolate, melted
2 egg whites, stiffly beaten
1 cup chopped pecans (optional)
1 unbaked (9-inch) pie shell

Mix the sugar, flour and salt in a bowl. Add the melted butter, egg yolks and vanilla, beating until smooth. Beat in the chocolate. Fold in the egg whites and the pecans. Pour into the pie shell. Bake at 325 degrees for 30 minutes. Cool to room temperature. Serve with vanilla ice cream.
Yield: 8 servings.

Hot Water Pastries

$^3/_4$ cup butter-flavored shortening
1 tablespoon milk
1 teaspoon salt
$^1/_4$ cup boiling water
2 cups plus 2 tablespoons all-purpose flour

Whip the shortening, milk and salt with a fork in a bowl until fluffy. Add the water, stirring until the consistency of whipped cream. Add the flour all at once, mixing until the mixture forms a ball; do not overmix. Roll into 2 circles between waxed paper. Fit each circle into a 9-inch pie plate. Trim and flute the edge. Bake at 425 degrees for 12 minutes or until brown.
Yield: 2 (9-inch) pie crusts.

Pecan Pie

This is a bit less sweet than most pecan pies.

1 cup sugar
¹/₂ cup light corn syrup
¹/₄ cup butter
3 eggs, beaten
¹/₄ teaspoon salt, or to taste
1 teaspoon vanilla extract
1 cup pecan pieces
1 unbaked (9-inch) pie shell

Bring the sugar, corn syrup and butter to a boil in a saucepan.
Beat the eggs in a large bowl. Stir in the sugar mixture. Add the salt,
vanilla and pecans, stirring until the pecans are coated. Pour into the pie
shell. Bake at 375 degrees for 35 to 40 minutes or until a knife
inserted near the center comes out clean.
Yield: 6 to 8 servings.

Low-Fat New York Cheesecake

1 recipe graham cracker pie shell
1 cup low-fat cottage cheese
2 pounds low-fat cream cheese, softened
1 cup sugar
2 eggs, slightly beaten
1 teaspoon vanilla extract
2 tablespoons cornstarch

Prepare the pie shell recipe and pat into a springform pan. Chill thoroughly.
Beat the cottage cheese in a bowl until smooth. Add the remaining
ingredients and mix well. Pour into the prepared pan. Bake at 450 degrees
for 10 minutes. Reduce the oven temperature to 200 degrees. Bake for 45
minutes longer or until lightly browned. Cool. Chill for 3 hours or longer.
Yield: 8 to 10 servings.

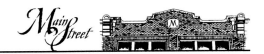

Yankee Doodle Apple Cobbler

5 large Granny Smith apples, peeled, thinly sliced
$^1/_2$ cup dried currants
$^1/_2$ cup chopped dates
$^1/_2$ cup golden raisins
$^1/_2$ cup chopped walnuts or pecans
$^1/_2$ cup apple juice
2 cups all-purpose flour
$^3/_4$ cup sugar
2 teaspoons baking powder
$^1/_2$ teaspoon salt
1 teaspoon cinnamon
$^1/_8$ teaspoon nutmeg
$^1/_3$ cup butter, softened
1 cup low-fat milk
1 cup apple juice

Arrange the apples in a greased 4-quart shallow baking dish.
Sprinkle the currants, dates, raisins and walnuts over the apples. Pour
$^1/_2$ cup apple juice over the fruit and nuts. Combine the flour, sugar,
baking powder, salt, cinnamon and nutmeg in a large bowl and mix well.
Cut in the butter until crumbly. Stir in the milk. Spoon the batter
over the apple mixture. Bring 1 cup apple juice to a boil in a saucepan. Pour
the juice over the batter. Bake at 350 degrees for $1^1/_4$ hours or until
the apple juice is absorbed. Serve over vanilla ice cream.
Yield: 12 to 15 servings.

Chocolate Almond Torte

1 (23-ounce) package brownie mix with chocolate chips
3 eggs
1/4 cup water
1 cup whipping cream
1/4 cup sifted confectioners' sugar
1/4 to 1/2 teaspoon almond extract
1/4 cup baking cocoa
3 tablespoons water
2 tablespoons vegetable oil
2 tablespoons light corn syrup
2 cups sifted confectioners' sugar
1/2 cup toasted sliced almonds

Combine the brownie mix, eggs and 1/4 cup water in a bowl and
mix well. Pour into 3 greased and floured 8-inch round baking pans. Bake
at 350 degrees for 12 minutes. Cool in the pans on a wire rack for
10 minutes. Remove to the wire rack to cool completely. Beat the whipping
cream at medium speed in a mixer bowl until foamy. Add 1/4 cup
confectioners' sugar gradually, beating until stiff. Stir in the almond extract.
Spread between the baked layers. Combine the cocoa, 3 tablespoons
water, oil and corn syrup in a saucepan. Cook over low heat for 2 minutes,
stirring constantly until smooth. Remove from the heat. Stir in
2 cups confectioners' sugar. Drizzle over the torte.
Decorate the side with the almonds.
Yield: 12 servings.

Old-Fashioned Banana Pudding

3 egg yolks
1 cup milk
3 (or more) bananas, sliced
1/2 package vanilla wafers
1 cup sugar
1/2 cup all-purpose flour
2 tablespoons margarine
1 teaspoon vanilla extract
3 egg whites
1/2 cup sugar

Beat the egg yolks with the milk in a double boiler. Cook over boiling water until heated through, stirring frequently. Cool slightly. Alternate layers of bananas and vanilla wafers in a 9x9-inch baking dish. Mix 1 cup of the sugar and the flour in a small bowl. Stir into the milk mixture. Cook over boiling water until thickened, stirring occasionally. Stir in the margarine and vanilla. Pour over the bananas and vanilla wafers. Beat the egg whites in a mixer bowl until soft peaks form. Add 1/2 cup sugar gradually, beating constantly until stiff. Spread over the custard, sealing to the edges. Bake at 400 degrees until the meringue is browned.

Yield: 6 to 8 servings.

Before the days of Shoney's, Dairy Queen and McDonald's, Franklin's fun restaurant was the Gilco, owned and operated in the 1950s by Nelle and A.B. Thomas. This was the local "hangout" and hamburger place for teenagers and adults alike. Nelle Thomas made all the desserts for the Gilco, and many Franklin residents will remember this as a favorite.

Amaretto Bread Pudding

$^3/_4$ cup raisins
1 loaf French bread, torn
1 quart half-and-half
3 eggs
1$^1/_2$ cups sugar
1 tablespoon almond extract
$^3/_4$ cup sliced almonds
$^1/_2$ cup unsalted butter
1 cup confectioners' sugar
1 egg, beaten
$^1/_4$ cup Amaretto

Place raisins in a small bowl; cover with warm water. Let stand for
30 minutes or until plump; drain. Combine the bread and half-and-half in
a bowl. Let stand, covered, for 1 hour. Beat 3 eggs, sugar and
almond extract in a small bowl. Fold in the bread mixture, raisins and
almonds. Spread evenly in a buttered 9x13-inch baking pan. Bake at
325 degrees for 50 minutes or until golden brown. Cool and cut into
squares. Cook the butter and confectioners' sugar in a double boiler over
boiling water until the confectioners' sugar is dissolved, stirring constantly,
do not boil. Remove from the heat. Whisk a small amount of the hot
mixture into the remaining egg; whisk the egg into the hot mixture.
Continue whisking until the sauce reaches room temperature. Stir in
the liqueur. Serve over the bread pudding.
Yield: 15 servings.

Flan

1¹/2 cups sugar
6 eggs, slightly beaten
¹/4 teaspoon salt
1 teaspoon vanilla extract
4 cups milk

Cook ¹/2 cup of the sugar in a heavy saucepan until syrupy and brown; do not burn. Pour into a 2-quart baking dish, covering the bottom evenly. Let stand until cool and set. Mix the remaining ingredients in a bowl. Pour through a strainer into the baking dish. Place the dish in a larger pan of hot water deep enough to come up side of dish 1 inch. Bake at 325 degrees for 1 hour or until a knife inserted near the center comes out clean. Remove from the oven and cool in the hot water until the custard reaches room temperature. Invert onto a serving dish to unmold.
Yield: 8 servings.

French Pudding

1¹/2 cups confectioners' sugar
¹/2 cup butter, softened
2 eggs
1 cup whipping cream
2 tablespoons confectioners' sugar
1 teaspoon vanilla extract
1 small package vanilla wafers, crushed
1 (8-ounce) can crushed pineapple
¹/2 cup toasted almonds

Cream 1¹/2 cups confectioners' sugar and the butter in a large mixer bowl until light and fluffy. Beat in the eggs. Beat the whipping cream with 2 tablespoons confectioners' sugar and the vanilla in a mixer bowl until stiff peaks form. Layer the wafer crumbs, egg mixture, undrained pineapple, whipped cream and almonds in a large serving dish. Chill until serving time.
Yield: 12 to 15 servings.

Amaretto Crème Over Fresh Fruit

Serve this delicious summer dessert in pretty crystal dessert dishes.

4 egg yolks, lightly beaten
1/2 cup sugar
2 tablespoons all-purpose flour
1 cup low-fat milk
1 tablespoon Amaretto
1/4 teaspoon vanilla extract
Sliced fresh peaches, raspberries, kiwifruit and strawberries

Combine the egg yolks, sugar and flour in a medium saucepan.
Add the milk gradually, stirring until smooth. Cook over low heat for 6 to 7
minutes or until a cooking thermometer reaches 160 degrees, stirring
constantly. Remove from the heat and stir in the liqueur and vanilla.
Cover and chill thoroughly. Spoon over the fruit in serving dishes.
Yield: 4 to 6 servings.

Chocolate Fondue

6 ounces unsweetened chocolate
1/2 cup butter
1 1/2 cups sugar
1 cup half-and-half
2 teaspoons vanilla extract

Melt the chocolate and butter in a saucepan over low heat. Add the
sugar, stirring until dissolved. Add the half-and-half gradually. Cook for 5
minutes or until thickened, stirring constantly. Beat in the vanilla.
Serve hot over fruit or pound cake.
Yield: 2 1/2 to 3 cups.

Restaurants & Bed & Breakfasts

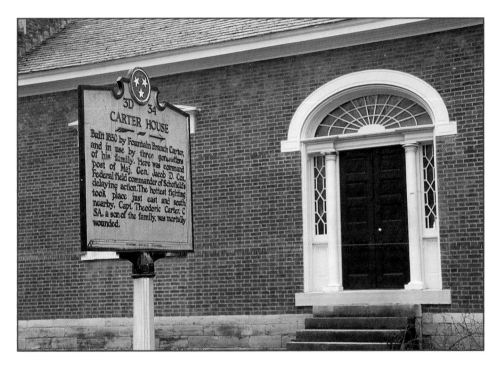

Carter House

Restaurants & Bed & Breakfasts

Carter House

The Carter House, renowned for its role at the center of the Battle of Franklin, was constructed in 1830. It is a Classic Revival home, with Doric ornamentation and parapet walls. While fierce fighting raged in the yard above them, the Carter family and several of their neighbors crouched in the basement with its thick stone walls. The home and its outbuildings have been restored as closely as possible to their pre-war state.

All three of the Carter sons were enlisted in the twentieth Tennessee Regiment in 1861. After being gone for over three years, Tod, the youngest son, was found wounded a short distance from his home by General Thomas Benton Smith. General Smith led Tod's father to where he was found wounded and Tod was taken back to the house, where he later died, while his family watched over him.

Carter House was purchased by the state in 1951. In 1961 the Carter House was designated as one of four sights in Tennessee of major importance to American History by the Register of Historic Landmarks. At 1140 Columbia Avenue, it is open daily to the public for guided tours.

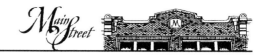

Pickled Peach Salad

*This has been a tried-and-true favorite of Choices
restaurant for the last ten years.*

1 (29-ounce) can sliced peaches in heavy syrup
$^1/_2$ cup vinegar
12 whole cloves
1 (6-ounce) package orange gelatin
2 cups boiling water
1 cup cold water

Drain the peaches, reserving the syrup. Chop the peaches and
set aside. Combine the reserved syrup, vinegar and cloves in a saucepan.
Bring to a boil. Stir in the peaches. Cool to room temperature. Chill for 24
hours or longer. Remove the cloves and drain the peaches. Dissolve the
gelatin in the boiling water in a bowl. Add the peaches and cold water. Pour
into a 9x12-inch glass dish. Chill until firm.
Yield: 12 servings.

CHOICES
**108 4th Avenue South
Franklin, Tennessee 37064**

Potato Casserole

This is an old-time favorite of Dotson's Restaurant.

3 pounds shredded frozen or fresh potatoes
1 small onion, diced
1 pound Colby cheese, shredded
1 (16-ounce) can chicken soup
1 teaspoon salt
1 teaspoon pepper

Combine the potatoes, onion, cheese, soup, salt and pepper in a
bowl and mix well. Pour into a greased 9x13-inch baking pan. Bake at 350
degrees for 40 minutes. Serve as is or place individual servings
on the grill to brown well on both sides.
Yield: 12 servings.

Good Home Cooking At It's Finest

RESTAURANT

Since 1943

Franklin, Tennessee
794-2805
or
794-2854

Spicy Shrimp

This is a pasta dish Franklin Chop House features as a "special," and although it is not a regular menu item, it is available all the time.

6 ounces linguini or fettuccini
Olive oil
1 tablespoon margarine
6 ounces shrimp, peeled, deveined
$^1/_2$ cup whipping cream
1 teaspoon Cajun seasoning, or to taste
1 tablespoon chopped scallions

Cook the linguini using the package directions and drain well. Stir in a small amount of olive oil. Wrap the linguini in plastic wrap and chill until needed. Heat the margarine in a sauté pan over medium-high heat. Add the shrimp. Cook until the shrimp turn pink, stirring constantly; do not overcook. Add the whipping cream, Cajun seasoning and pasta, stirring to mix evenly. Cook until the sauce begins to thicken, stirring constantly. Remove the pasta with tongs to a serving bowl. Pour the shrimp and sauce over the pasta. Top with the scallions. Serve immediately. It is best to cook no more than 2 servings at a time in the same sauté pan.
Yield: 1 serving.

1101 Murfreesboro Road • Franklin, Tennessee 37064

Green's Grocery Peach Cobbler

1 (16-ounce) can or 2 cups fresh peaches
1 (21-ounce) can peach pie filling
1 teaspoon cinnamon
$1/4$ cup sugar
1 cup all-purpose flour
1 cup sugar
2 teaspoons baking powder
$3/4$ to 1 cup milk
$1/2$ cup butter

Mix the peaches, pie filling, cinnamon and $1/4$ cup sugar in
a large bowl. Mix the flour, 1 cup sugar, baking powder and milk in a
medium bowl. Melt the butter in a baking pan. Pour the flour mixture over
the butter. Spoon the peach mixture over the flour mixture. Bake at 350
degrees for 30 to 40 minutes or until bubbly and heated through.
Yield: 8 servings.

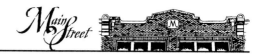

Herbert's Chess Pie

*Carolyn Dodson, manager of Herbert's Bar-B-Q Restaurant, says they
make on average 600 tarts per week. These tarts and her
Corn Light Bread are her most requested items.*

1 tablespoon apple cider vinegar
1 tablespoon light corn syrup
1 teaspoon vanilla extract
$1/2$ cup melted butter or margarine
1 cup sugar
4 eggs, slightly beaten
1 tablespoon bourbon (optional)
8 unbaked tart shells

Combine the vinegar, corn syrup, vanilla and melted butter in
a medium bowl and mix well. Combine the sugar and butter mixture in a
large bowl, stirring until well blended. Add the eggs and mix well. Stir in
the bourbon. Pour into the tart shells. Bake at 350 degrees for 25 to
30 minutes or until a knife inserted near the centers comes
out clean. Cool on a wire rack. May be prepared in a 9-inch
pie shell and baked for 35 to 40 minutes.
Yield: 8 servings.

Herbert's
Bar-B-Q Restaurant

Dine-In
Drive-Thru
Carry-Out
Catering

"Ya'll Come To See Us"

A Great Place To Eat In Historic Franklin
OPEN 7 DAYS — 10:00 A.M.
111 N. Royal Oaks Blvd.   Hwy. 96 & I-65
Franklin, Tennessee 37067
(located next to McDonald's)
Exit 65 on I-65
(615) 791-0700

Chocolate Meringue Pie

Merridee's Bread Basket is famous for this recipe. Still served every Friday at the bakery, this pie goes quickly and is a favorite of chocolate lovers everywhere.

$^1/_4$ cup butter
$^1/_4$ cup baking cocoa
$1^1/_2$ cups sugar
$^1/_3$ teaspoon salt
1 (12-ounce) can evaporated milk
3 egg yolks, slightly beaten
1 baked (9-inch) pie shell
$^1/_2$ cup egg whites
$^1/_4$ teaspoon cream of tartar
$^1/_2$ cup sugar

Melt the butter in a saucepan. Stir in the baking cocoa. Add $1^1/_2$ cups sugar and the salt and mix well. Add the evaporated milk gradually, stirring until mixed. Bring to a boil over moderate heat. Add half the hot mixture gradually to the egg yolks; add the egg yolks to the hot mixture. Return to a boil. Boil for 2 minutes, stirring frequently. Pour into the pie shell. Beat the egg whites and cream of tartar at high speed in a mixer bowl until foamy. Add $^1/_2$ cup sugar 1 tablespoon at a time, beating constantly until the mixture is stiff and has a dull glossy appearance. Spread over the pie filling, sealing to the edge. Bake at 325 degrees for 10 minutes or until the meringue is golden brown.
Yield: 6 to 8 servings.

Merridee's Bread Basket
Bakery and Restaurant

110 Fourth Avenue South
Franklin, TN 37064
(615) 790-3755

Remoulade Sauce

This sauce is what "makes" the Shrimp Salad at Nooley's.

2 egg yolks
$^1/_4$ cup vegetable oil
$^1/_4$ cup chopped fresh parsley
$^1/_2$ cup finely grated horseradish
$^1/_4$ lemon, seeded
2 tablespoons Creole mustard
2 tablespoons catsup
2 tablespoons Worcestershire sauce
1 tablespoon red wine vinegar
1 tablespoon Tabasco sauce
2 teaspoons paprika
1 teaspoon salt

Beat the egg yolks in a blender or food processor for 2 minutes.
Add the oil in a thin stream, processing constantly. Add the remaining
ingredients 1 at a time, processing until well mixed. Chill thoroughly.
Yield: 1$^1/_2$ cups.

German Apple Pancake

While this creation bakes it creates steam, resulting in a puffy pancake, golden and crisp on the outside, soft and "eggy" on the inside. Sliced fresh pears or peaches may be used instead of apples.

1 cup milk
3 eggs, at room temperature
3/4 cup all-purpose flour
2 tablespoons sugar
2 tablespoons butter
2 medium apples, peeled, cut into 1/4-inch slices
1/4 teaspoon cinnamon
1 tablespoon sugar
Confectioners' sugar

Combine the milk, eggs, flour and 2 tablespoons sugar in a medium bowl and whisk until mixed. Melt the butter over medium-high heat in a large heavy ovenproof skillet. Add the apples, cinnamon and 1 tablespoon sugar. Reduce the heat to medium. Cook for 2 to 3 minutes or until the apples are slightly softened, stirring occasionally. Remove from the heat. Pour the batter over the apples. Bake at 375 degrees for 30 to 35 minutes or until lightly browned and puffy. Cut into wedges and sprinkle with confectioners' sugar.
Yield: 6 to 8 servings.

Blueberry Hill
Bed and Breakfast
4591 Peytonsville Road
Franklin, TN 37064

Stuffed Avocado Salad

2 cups chopped cooked shrimp
$^1/_2$ cup minced onion
2 tablespoons freshly squeezed lemon juice
2 tablespoons chopped fresh cilantro
$^1/_2$ teaspoon salt
$^1/_2$ teaspoon white pepper
$^3/_4$ cup Thousand Island salad dressing
2 avocados, cut into halves
Lemon slices and parsley for garnish

Combine the shrimp, onion, lemon juice, cilantro, salt and
white pepper in a bowl and mix well. Stir in the salad dressing.
Stuff the mixture into the avocado halves. Chill until serving time.
Garnish with lemon slices and parsley.
Yield: 2 to 4 servings.

The Courtney House Bed and Breakfast
515 Church Street
Franklin, Tennessee
(615) 791-0237

Carrot Casserole

2 cups mashed cooked carrots
1 cup sugar
2 tablespoons all-purpose flour
1 teaspoon baking powder
$^1/_2$ cup margarine
3 eggs, beaten
$^1/_8$ teaspoon cinnamon, or to taste

Combine the carrots, sugar, flour, baking powder, margarine and
eggs in a bowl and mix well. Spoon into a 2-quart casserole. Sprinkle with
the cinnamon. Bake, covered, at 400 degrees for 15 minutes. Reduce the
oven temperature to 350 degrees. Bake, uncovered, for 45 minutes or until
a knife inserted near the center comes out clean.
Yield: 6 to 8 servings.

English Manor
❖
A Bed & Breakfast Inn
&
Catering Service

6304 Murray Lane
Brentwood, Tennessee 37027-6210
Willia Dean English, Owner/Innkeeper
☎
(Phones Answered 24 Hours)
(615) 373-4627
(615) 373-4640
For Making Reservations Only
1-800-332-4640

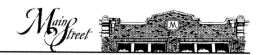

Attention Shrimp

1 1/2 tablespoons Creole Seafood Seasoning (see below)
1 1/2 tablespoons paprika
1/2 cup melted unsalted butter
1 pound large shrimp

Combine the Creole Seafood Seasoning and paprika in a small bowl.
Combine half the mixture with the butter in a medium bowl. Dip the
shrimp in the mixture to coat. Arrange the shrimp in a single layer in a
large foil-lined pan. Pour any remaining butter mixture over the shrimp.
Broil near the heat source for 5 minutes or until the shrimp turn pink.
Sprinkle with the remaining seasoning mixture. Broil for 30 seconds.
Arrange the shrimp seasoning side up on a serving plate. Serve
the pan drippings as a dipping sauce for bread. May be served
as an entrée over pasta al dente.
Yield: 4 to 6 servings.

Lyric Springs Country Inn
7306 South Harpeth Road / Franklin, Tennessee 37064
(615) 779-3383 or 1-800-621-7824

Creole Seafood Seasoning

1 tablespoon sweet paprika
1 tablespoon salt
2 teaspoons onion powder
2 teaspoons garlic powder
1 teaspoon cayenne
1 teaspoon white pepper
1 teaspoon black pepper
2 teaspoons dried thyme
2 teaspoons dried basil

Combine all the ingredients in a bowl and mix well.
Store in a tightly covered container.
Yield: 1/2 cup.

Yellow Squash Casserole

3 pounds fresh or frozen yellow squash, sliced
1 large onion, sliced
2 cups water
$^1/_2$ cup butter
15 soda crackers, crushed
1 pound Velveeta cheese, cut into small pieces
2 tablespoons sugar
$^1/_2$ teaspoon salt
1 teaspoon pepper

Combine the squash, onion and water in a saucepan. Cook
until tender. Remove from the heat and drain well. Add the butter, crackers,
cheese, sugar, salt and pepper and mix well. Pour into a greased baking
dish. Bake at 325 degrees until light golden brown.
Yield: 10 to 12 servings.

BARN • BED
BREAKFAST

FRANKLIN, TN

Lemon-Honey Chicken

1 broiler, cut up, or 2 to 3 chicken breasts
$^1/_4$ cup vegetable oil
$^1/_4$ cup honey
1 egg yolk
2 tablespoons lemon juice
2 tablespoons soy sauce
1 teaspoon paprika
$^1/_4$ teaspoon nutmeg

Rinse the chicken and pat dry. Arrange in a foil-lined 9x13-inch baking pan. Combine the oil, honey, egg yolk, lemon juice, soy sauce, paprika and nutmeg in a bowl and mix well. Pour over the chicken, coating each piece. Bake at 350 degrees for 45 to 60 minutes or until the chicken is cooked through, turning the chicken and basting with the sauce 1 to 2 times.
Yield: 4 servings.

A LUXURY COUNTRY INN
6994 Giles Hill Road
College Grove, Tennessee 37046

Sweet Annie's

Bed, Breakfast & Barn

7201 Crow Cut Road, S.W.
Fairview, Tennessee 37062
615-799-8833
Fax 615-799-0777

Sweet Annie's French Toast

4 eggs, beaten
1/2 cup (or more) milk
Butternut extract to taste
Cinnamon to taste
6 ounces cream cheese, softened
8 slices cinnamon-raisin bread
2 to 3 bananas, sliced
Orange Sauce (see below)
Fresh orange slices for garnish

Mix the eggs, milk, butternut extract and cinnamon in a bowl.
Spread cream cheese over 4 slices of bread. Top with the bananas and the
remaining bread slices. Dip in the milk mixture. Brown the sandwiches on
both sides in a skillet. Serve with Orange Sauce or maple syrup.
Garnish with fresh orange slices.
Yield: 4 servings.

Orange Sauce

3/4 cup orange juice
1 tablespoon sugar
2 tablespoons orange liqueur

Combine the orange juice, sugar and liqueur in a saucepan. Boil
for several minutes or until slightly thickened, stirring occasionally.

Menus

Liberty Hall

Menus

Liberty Hall

Liberty Hall was built in 1903 by R. W. McLemore. It is of the Classical Revival style, which often represents a combination of various classical styles and contemporary elements. This style of home appeared during the late 1800s and early 1900s. From an era when living was grand, this home gives the feel of a Victorian mansion. This very formal home features five bedrooms, four bathrooms, maid quarters on the third floor, and a carriage house with butler's quarters.

Mr. McLemore named his home Liberty Hall because his children would often bring lots of friends home with them from college "on liberty." With over five thousand square feet of living space, this spacious home could accommodate many house guests, and provide a welcome retreat from life on campus.

This lovely home can be found at 902 West Main Street in the Hincheyville Historic District, and is beautifully maintained by its current owner, Mrs. Frieda Jenkins-Smith.

Menus

Brunch

Sausage and Mushroom Casserole
page 98

Garlic Cheese Grits
page 101

Autumn Apple Bake
page 100

Morning Glory Muffins
page 129

Champagne Punch
page 28

Symphony on the Lawn

Make-Ahead Fruit Salad
page 53

Broccoli Salad
page 56

Chicken and Mango Chutney Salad
page 110

Marshmallow Brownies
page 149

Tea Punch
page 29

Unexpected Company Special!

Chicory Salad
page 58

Grilled Teriyaki Salmon
page 89

Couscous with Vegetables
page 136

Magnificent Cheese Muffins
page 128

Apricot Nectar Cake
page 144

Menus

Mother's Sunday Dinner

Grilled Marinated Chuck Roast
page 68

Green Bean Bundles
page 136

Green-Moore House Corn Pudding
page 135

Never-Fail Rolls
page 130

Million Dollar Pound Cake with Chocolate Fondue
pages 147 and 162

Fourth of July Celebration

Glazed Spareribs
page 75

Tangy Coleslaw
page 59

Hot Baked Beans
page 133

"Miss Sarah's" Corn Light Bread
page 123

Yankee Doodle Apple Cobbler
page 157

Main Street Festival Get-Together

Pork Tenderloin with Wine Sauce
page 73

Roasted Potato Salad
page 140

Apricot Bread
page 125

French Pudding
page 161

For the Wild

Minnesota Wild Rice Soup
page 41

Phyllo Chicken
page 88

Carrot Casserole
pages 134 or 174

Fudge Pie in Hot Water Pastry
page 155

Menus

A Jazzy Meal

Tomato and Cucumber Salad
page 63

Baked Shrimp with Roasted Peppers and Cheese
page 90

Citrus Rice
page 118

Onion and Cheese Bread
page 128

Flan
page 161

Dinner by Candlelight

Marian's Mushrooms
page 16

Caesar Salad
page 57

Roast Beef Tenderloin with Horseradish Sauce
page 67

Roasted Orange Potatoes
page 139

Cheese Pepper Bread
page 127

Pecan Pie
page 156

An Elegant Spring Dinner

Mixed Greens with Rosemary Vinaigrette
page 60

Roast Leg of Lamb
page 79

Mashed Potatoes and Parsnips with Parsley
page 139

Baby Carrots with Tarragon Glaze
page 135

Parmesan Crescents
page 122

Lemon Chess Pie
page 154

Bibliography

"A Walking Tour of Downtown Franklin." Historic Preservation Program and the Center for Historic Preservation at Middle Tennessee State University. 1985.

Bowman, Virginia McDaniel. *Historic Williamson County: Old Homes and Sites.* 1971.

Franklin: A Photographic Recollection. Franklin National Bank and Bob and Jackie Canady, 1989.

"National Register Properties: Williamson County, Tennessee." Edited by Jeri McLeland Hasselbring, Mary Pearce and Richard Warwick. Published by The Heritage Foundation of Franklin and Williamson County, The Williamson County Historical Society, and Williamson County Tourism. 1995.

"St. Paul's Church, Franklin." *Tennessee Historical Quarterly.* Spring 1975.

Williamson County: A Pictorial History. James A. Crutchfield. 1980.

Photography

For over thirty years the name Sam Causey has been synonymous
with excellence in photographic technique. The art is
practiced with skill, respect and deliberation . . . this requires
the rare combination of an artist, a professional technician
and a practitioner who loves and is dedicated to his craft.

A couple of years ago Sam convinced the husband and wife
team of Ernie and Lorraine Johnson to join his studio. It has proven to
be a perfect union. Ernie and Lorraine each owned and operated
their own studios before their marriage. Each have wonderfully warm
personalities and a deep love for photography. Their list of
photographic degrees and honors would fill a small book. They are
loved and admired by their peers and their clients. They
both hold the degree of "Master of Photography."

Please enjoy the evidence of their excellence through the
photographs they have created for this book.

Recipe Contributors

Mrs. James Houston Akin (Pug)

Mrs. K. Edward Alexander (Judy)

Ms. Mary Jane Anderson

Mrs. Greg Andress (Joann)

Mrs. Mike Argo (Heather)

Mrs. Dan Armfield (Nancy)

Mrs. John Arnold (Jill)

Mrs. John Arnold (Saundra)

Mrs. John L. Barker (Margaret)

Mrs. Paul Barlar (Gail)

Mrs. Larry Barnhill (Judy)

Mrs. Jim Barraza (Cindy)

Mrs. Mark Basenberg (Martha)

Ms. Tammy Bass

Mrs. Kenny Beam (Wendy)

Mrs. Earl Bentz (Janet)

Mrs. Deweese Berry IV (Kathy)

Mrs. James D. Berry (Jackie)

Mrs. Tyler Berry (Nancy)

Mrs. Chuck Blackburn (Marsha)

Mrs. Milton Blair (Sharon)

Blueberry Hill Bed and Breakfast (Joan Reesman)

Mrs. Fred Bohlen (Trisha)

Mrs. Joe Bowman (Virginia)

Mrs. Joseph Bowman (Gilda)

Mrs. Shelby Boyd

Mrs. Craig Brent (Susan)

Mrs. Jerry B. Brinkley (Gayle)

Mrs. Charles L. Brooks (Penny)

Mrs. Jim Brubaker (Nancy)

Mrs. John Bufford (Rose)

Mrs. Betsy Burnett

Mrs. Ken Caldwell (Tina)

Mrs. Shawn Carder (Macie)

Mrs. Frank Carlton (Jan)

Mrs. Robert Caruthers (Valleau)

Mrs. Leonard Cathey (Ruth)

Choices Restaurant

Mrs. David Clark (Sara)

Mrs. Willie Clark (Debby)

Ms. Nancy P. Conway

Mrs. Billy Cook (Ruthie)

Mrs. Ellis Cook (Carolyn)

Mrs. Tim Corl (Patti)

The Courtney House Bed and Breakfast (Kamy and Alexandra Kheshtenejad)

Mrs. Tommy Crocker (Ann)

Mrs. Herbert Crockett (Peggy)

Mrs. Harvey Crouch (Elise)

Mrs. Tim Curtin (Sherri)

Mrs. Greg Daily (Collie)

Mrs. Elizabeth Daniel

Mrs. Jimmy Darnell (Sherri)

Mrs. Patrick D'Eramo (Christine)

Mrs. Grady DeVan (Ann)

Ms. Janie Diemer

Mrs. Earle M. Dorset (Dee)

Dotson's Restaurant (Art McCloud)

Mrs. Michael Dray (Barbara)

Mrs. Hugh DuPree (Pat)

Mrs. Chuck Echols (Cyndi)

Mrs. Rex Edmonds (Connie)

English Manor Bed and Breakfast (Willia Dean English)

Mrs. Leonard Erhridge (Louise)

Mrs. William Eubank III (Carolyn)

Mrs. William P. Eubank (Alma)

Mrs. David Evans (René)

Mrs. Mark Feemster (Christine)

Mrs. Everett Floyd (Ann)

Mrs. George John Forbes (Barbara)

Mrs. Alton Fox (Betty)

Mrs. John Fox (Elaine)

Mrs. John Fox (Frances)

Mrs. Randy Fox (Debbie)

Mrs. Wayne Fox (Margaret)

Franklin Chop House

Mrs. Dennis Franklin (Jennifer)

Mrs. John Franklin (Diane)

Mrs. Gary Frazier (Rana)

Mrs. Mark A. Funderburg (Sue)

Mrs. John N. Gant (Jennie)

Mrs. Kevin Garland (Pam)

Mrs. James Garrett (Barbara)

Mrs. Donald Garrison (Nancy)

Ms. Jeanne Gatlin

Ms. Sue Gatlin

Mrs. John Gauld (Pam)

Mrs. Patricia Greene Gayden

Mrs. James Geraughty, Sr. (Charlotte)

Mrs. Huey Gibbs (Tammy)

Mr. Jim Gibbs

Mrs. George Gochanour (Naomi)

Mrs. Mike Godwin (Rosemary)

Mrs. Will Gold (Kristen)

Ms. Elizabeth Gourieux

Green's Grocery (Aubrey Preston)

Mrs. Johnny Gregory (Lisa)

Mrs. Wayne Gregory (Kathryn)

Mrs. James R. Grotte (Susan)

Mrs. John Hackney (Ann)

Mrs. Dan Halford (Julia)

Mrs. David Hall (Brenda)

Mrs. Richard Hall, Jr. (Jill)

Mrs. Richard Hall, Sr. (Sonya)

Mrs. Scott Hall (Carolyn)

Mrs. Ron Hamby (Donna)

Mrs. Wade Harley (Delores)

Mrs. Tom Harmon (Peggy)

Mrs. George Harris (Frances)

Mrs. Allen Henry (Paris)

Herbert's Bar-B-Q Restaurant (Carolyn Dodson)

Mrs. John Hiatt (Nancy)

Mrs. Mike Hill (Karen)

Mrs. Michael Hitchcock (Betty)

Mrs. Olney Hitchcock (Robbie)

Mrs. Scott Holmes (Marlene)

Mrs. Garland Honeycutt (Jeanne)

Mrs. Joe Horne (Pam)

Mrs. Scott House (Kris)

Mrs. Chance Hughes (Linda)

Mrs. David Hughes (Trish)

Mrs. Don Hughes (Libby)

Mrs. Bill Hurt (Linda)

Mrs. Donald Husi (Rebecca)

Inn Towne Bed and Breakfast (Debra Patton)

Mrs. Shearer Irvin (Susie)

Mrs. Eddy Jackson (Susie)

Ms. Eulalie Jefferson

Mrs. Bobby Joe Jenkins (Nellie Bee)

Mrs. David Johnson (Janet)

Mrs. Douglas Jones (Missy)

Mrs. Peter Jordan (Rudy)

Mrs. Chris Keffer (Stephanie)

Mrs. Jack Kelley (Boots)

Mrs. James E. Kelly (Tawna)

Mrs. Ben Kilgore (Sarah)

Mrs. Dennis King (Merrie)

Mrs. Clifton Kirby (Sharon)

Mrs. Charles Kraft (Judy)

Mrs. Richard Lane (Susan)

Mrs. Bobby Langley (Mary Ann)

Mrs. Doug Langston (Jane)

Mrs. Frank Lashlee (Sandra)

Mrs. Brooks Layman (Elise)

Mrs. Calvin Lehew (Marilyn)

Mrs. Edward Lewis (Elecia)

Mrs. Jeff Lewis (Connie)

Ms. Mary Frances Ligon

Mrs. Ronald S. Ligon (Marty)

Mrs. Jerry Lillard (Karen)

Mrs. Jimmy Lillard (Sara)

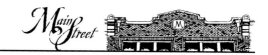

Ms. Kaye Lindsey
Mrs. Joel Locke (Frieda)
Mrs. John Loughran (Marian)
Mrs. Brad Lukens (Liz)
Mrs. Drew Luna (Tina)
Lyric Springs Country Inn
    (Patsy Bruce)
Mrs. Sidney Maddox (Dorothy)
Mrs. Mark Maddox (Lorenda)
Mrs. Herman Major
    (Lula Fain)
Mrs. John Maloof (Kris)
Mrs. Ron Martin (Mona)
Mrs. Herbert McCall (Nella)
Mrs. Lewis McCarver (Patti)
Mrs. John M. McCord
    (Kathryn)
Mrs. Rick McKnight (Cathy)
Ms. Debbie McMillian
Mrs. Mike McPherson (Lisa)
Mrs. John Meadows (Kathy)
Mrs. Stan D. Meers (Tyna)
Mrs. Terry W. Merrell (Lucy)
Merridee's Breadbasket
    (Marilyn J. Kreider)
Mrs. Phillip Miller (Nancy)
Mrs. Michael Mills (Martha)
Miss Jerri's Restaurant
    (Jerri Pruitt)
Mrs. Pete Misrr (Melinda)
Mrs. Adolphus Mitchell
    (Virginia)
Mrs. Tom Mitchell (Joan)
Ms. Ruth Molitor
Mrs. Gene Monger (Betty)
Mrs. Charles Moodespaugh
    (Karen)
Mrs. Ed Moody (Eileen)
Mrs. Rick Moody (Nancy)
Mrs. Gary Moore (Audrey)
Mrs. John Moore (Sherrie)
Ms. Ann Moran
Mrs. John M. Morris (Joy)
Mrs. William Mott (Courtney)
Mrs. Rocky Myers (Carla)

Namaste Acres Barn, Bed and
    Breakfast (Lisa Winters)
Mrs. Don Nix (Katrina)
Mrs. Billy Noland (Barbara)
Nooley's (Sandy Elder)
Mrs. Ira M. Norman (Naomi)
Mrs. Craig North (Sheryl)
Mrs. Steven O'Connor-Lieber
    (Katie)
Mrs. T. J. O'Connor (Kelly)
Mrs. Bill Omar (Pam)
Mrs. Mark Orme (Lori)
Mrs. Robert Osburn (Merrian)
Mrs. Joseph A. Otterpohl
    (Barbie)
Mrs. Robert Pacholski
    (Lenny)
Mrs. Todd Panther (Cheryl)
Mrs. John Parish (Lucile)
Mrs. Dan Parker (Cathy)
Mrs. Sara Parks
Mrs. Jackson Parr
    (Millie Bergeron)
Dolly Parton
Ms. Debra Patton
Peacock Hill Country Inn
    (Anita Ogilvie)
Mrs. Eric Peterson (Jenni)
Mrs. Tom Peterson (June)
Mrs. James G. Petway
    (Willodene)
Mrs. Jim Petway (Terri)
Mrs. Norman A. Peyronnin
    (Trudy)
Mrs. Estelle Pinkerton
Mrs. Ken Premo (Kim)
Mrs. Steve Priest (Sheila)
Mrs. David Randall (Melinda)
Mrs. Mark Randall (Laurie)
Mrs. James Roberts (Margaret)
Mrs. E. A. Robertson (Rose)
Mrs. Miller Rucker
    (Annelle)
Mrs. Michael Samford
    (Monica)

Mrs. Wert Sanders
    (Willa Frances)
Mrs. Tim Sawyer (Denise)
Mrs. Ted Schilling (Mindy)
Mrs. David Schumacher
    (Karen)
Mrs. David Seiberling (Sara)
Mrs. Joseph Sessions (Lisa)
Mrs. Zach Shappley (Janet)
Mrs. Oswald Shaw (Christene)
Mrs. Steve Shearer (Cindy)
Mrs. John Sheldon (Pam)
Mrs. James M. Shull
    (Carol Ann)
Mrs. C. Cloy Simmons (M. E.)
Mrs. Randy Sims (Kelly)
Mrs. Richard Sims (Debbie)
Mrs. Jim Sipes (Melody)
Mrs. John R. Slavin (Jenny)
Mrs. John P. Slayden (Janet)
Mrs. Kevin R. Smith (Vicki)
Mrs. Michael W. Smith
    (Debbie)
Mrs. Neal Smith (Joan)
Mrs. Paul Smith (Inge)
Mrs. Gwen Spann
Mrs. Collins Spaulding
    (Collins)
Mrs. Nathan Spaulding (Jo)
Mrs. John Spelman (Jodie)
Mrs. Don Spurgeon (Ruth)
Mrs. Hal Stafford (Alice)
Mrs. Scott Stewart (Kim)
Mrs. Blaine Strock (Cindy)
Mrs. Richard Srults (Jennifer)
Mrs. Chris Sullivan (Terri)
Mrs. Lawrence Sullivan
    (Candy)
Sweet Annie's Bed and
    Breakfast (Ann M. Murphy)
Mrs. Glen Switzer (Sheri)
Mrs. Mark Thessin (Margie)
Mrs. Dale Thomas (Jennifer)
Mrs. David Thompson (Kim)
Mrs. Juanita Tollison

Mrs. Robert E. Torbert, Jr.
    (Tina)
Mrs. Dick Tracy (Susan)
Mrs. Michael Tramontana
    (Maryanne)
Mrs. Richard Triggs (Heidi)
Mrs. H. Thomas Tripp (Fran)
Mrs. Jimmy Turnbow (Ruth)
Mrs. Connie Turvy
Mrs. Thomas L. Van Dyke, Jr.
    (Laureen)
Mrs. Jewell VanHooser
Mrs. Owen Waldrop, Jr.
    (Becky)
Mrs. Tommy Walker
    (Minnie Lee)
Mrs. Timothy G. Wallace
    (Rhonda R.)
Mrs. William S. Walton (Patti)
Mrs. Charles Warden (Cheryl)
Mrs. Steve Wariner (Caryn)
Mrs. Marion Warren
Mrs. Rick Warwick (Elaine)
Mrs. James A. Waters (Alberta)
Mrs. B. G. Watson (Jane)
Mrs. John Watson (Connie)
Mrs. Bruce Weathers (Connie)
Mrs. Richard H. Wells
    (Sharon)
Mrs. Mark J. Werner (Debbie)
Ms. Adrienne West
Mrs. Roger West (Kati)
Mrs. Larry Westbrook (Candie)
Mrs. Adam Wieck (Beth)
Mrs. Jim Wieck (Judy)
Mrs. Alison D. Williams
    (Cathy)
Mrs. Sam Williams (Evelyn)
Mrs. Ridley Wills (Irene)
Mrs. William E. Wood (Leah)
Mrs. G. Eddy Woodard
    (Bonnie)
Ms. Ragan York
Mrs. Vicki York

Index

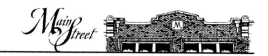

Order Information

Main Street

A Tasteful Passage Through Historic Franklin

Junior Auxiliary of Franklin
P.O. Box 541
Franklin, Tennessee 37065-0541

Please send _____ copies of *Main Street* @ $19.95 each _____

Sales tax $1.75 each _____

Plus postage and handling of $3.00 each _____

Total _____

Make checks payable to: JAF

Name _____

Address _____

City _____ State _____ Zip Code _____

Telephone Number _____

___ Please send information about our companion cookbook *Flaunting Our Finest*.
___ Please send information on becoming a member of Junior Auxiliary of Franklin.

Main Street

A Tasteful Passage Through Historic Franklin

Junior Auxiliary of Franklin
P.O. Box 541
Franklin, Tennessee 37065-0541

Please send _____ copies of *Main Street* @ $19.95 each _____

Sales tax $1.75 each _____

Plus postage and handling of $3.00 each _____

Total _____

Make checks payable to: JAF

Name _____

Address _____

City _____ State _____ Zip Code _____

Telephone Number _____

___ Please send information about our companion cookbook *Flaunting Our Finest*.
___ Please send information on becoming a member of Junior Auxiliary of Franklin.

Photocopied orders accepted.